Floreat Lewys

Five Hundred Years of Lewes Old Grammar School

LEWES GRAMMAR SCHOOL.

MIDSUMMER EXAMINATION, 1860.

ARITHMETIC.

1. ultiply 18073 by 621, and divide the product by 207.

2. ultiply 18 miles 3 furlongs 27 po 2 yards by 621, and divide by 207.

3. How many persons can receive £1 10s. 4½d. out of a sum of £66,307 12s. 7½d. ?

4. Find, by the rule of practice, the v lue of 6426 articles at 10s 6¼d. each ?

5. If 17 men earn £249 18s. 0d. in 21 weeks, in what time will 19 men earn £438 18s. 0d. ?

6. Reduce to its simplest terms $\dfrac{\frac{2}{3} - \frac{3}{4}}{4\frac{4}{7} - 3\frac{3}{9}}$

7. Reduce 4s. 4½d. to the fraction of s. 10d.

8. If A can reap ⅘ of a field in 2⅔ days, and B can reap ¾ of it in 4½ days, in what time can A and B reap the whole field together?

9. If a wall 320 feet long, 9 feet high, and 22½ inches thick be built by 10 men in 45 days of 12 hours each, in how many days of 14 hours each would 60 men build a wall 14 feet high, and 2¼ feet thick, round a park 8½ miles in circumference ?

10. Find the value of $\dfrac{3.0005 \times .006}{.0009}$

11. Add together the circulating decimals .1£ and .02£, and divide the sum by .04£.

12. A offers to give £2. 3s. 4d. for every pound B gives; B gives £5. 6s. 8d., what what will A have to give?

13. The value of 1 oz. Troy of English standard gold is £3. 17s. 10½d. ; 31.1 French grammes are equal in weight to 1 oz. Troy, the worth of a given weight of English standard gold is to that of an equal weight of French standard gold as 91.5 : 90, and 1 gramme of French gold is worth 3.1 francs. Required the value of £1. in francs.

14. Extract the square root of 4142689, and of .121 to three places of decimals.

15. What is the discount on £981. 8s. 4d. for 97 days at 3½ per cent. per annum ?

16. What rate of interest arises from money vested in 7 per cent. stock at £175 ?

17. Bought £13. 6s. 8d. worth of apples at 3s. 4d. per bushel. part of which being damaged, were entirely lost : for the rest, which were sold at 50 per cent. profit, I received £16; how many bushels were damaged ?

18. how many years will £12. amount to £27. at 5 per cent. compound interest ?

19. istern is 7 feet 6 inches long, 1 oot 9 inches broad, and 3 feet 6 how many llons of water will it contain ?

20. e length of a hollow roller is 4 feet, the exterior diameter is thickness of the metal ¾ inch; what is its solidity ?

21. he area of a regular hexagon is 14 square feet, required the length its side.

A Lewes Grammar School maths paper from 1860. How well would you have done?

Floreat Lewys

Five Hundred Years of Lewes Old Grammar School

David Arscott

"It has survived a civil war, two world wars and outlived no fewer than twenty-one kings and queens . . ."

– *BBC TV news report on the LOGS quincentenary*

Front cover painting © Rupert Denyer
Back cover photograph: Founder's Day Parade 2012 © Jim Holden
Endpapers © Jane Dinmore

Published by Pomegranate Press,
Dolphin House, 51 St Nicholas Lane, Lewes, Sussex BN7 2JZ
pomegranatepress@aol.com
www.pomegranate-press.co.uk

ISBN: 978–1–907242–33–5

British Library Cataloguing-in-Publication Data.
A catalogue record for this book is available from the British Library

Printed and bound by Ashford Colour Press, Gosport, Hampshire PO13 0FW

Contents

Acknowledgements

A great many people have contributed to the historical part of this book, not least among them the former pupils and members of staff whose names appear in its pages and who have supplied both memories and memorabilia. Those otherwise unsung, but who have given the author various invaluable kinds of help, include Judy Brent, Diana Crook, Esme Evans, John Hecks, Paul Lucas, Viola Lyons, Graham Mayhew, Mike Norgrove, Bruce Parker and Carrie Whyte.

The illustrations derive from a variety of sources and LOGS wishes to thank the following for their kind permission:

The British Library for the illustrated manuscript on page 17, the page from John Evelyn's *Elysium Brittanicum* on page 23, John Buckler's 1830 drawing of the grammar school on page 29 and the portraits on pages 31, 32 and 33.

Bob Cairns for the postcards on pages 71 and 73.

The *Daily Mail* for the Jon cartoon on page 103.

John Davey for the postcard on page 69.

East Sussex Record Office [ESRO] for Agnes Morley's will on page 13 (AMS 5996/1/7); the plans and architects' drawings on pages 61 and 62 (DL/A/25/138) and on pages 72–73 (DL/A/25/531); the posters on pages 64 and 66 (DL/D/197/1); the postcard on page 70 (ACC 3670/1/5) and the playbill on page 54 (AMS 6005/31).

John Houghton for the plan of the Grange on page 14.

Dom Ramos for the imaginative creation of John Streeter's likeness on page 24: 'He wears the blue sash and tan jerkin of a New Model Army officer.'

Sherborne Abbey for the misericord on page 17.

Surrey Archaeological Society for the John Evelyn portrait on page 21, from an original picture by Sir Godfrey Kneller.

Sussex Archaeological Society for the poster on page 37, the painting of the Lewes avalanche on page 40 and the reunion document on page 82.

Trinity College School, Port Hope, Canada for the portrait of Charles Badgley on page 57.

The endpapers of the book were designed and produced by Jane Dinmore, head of art at the school's senior department.

The gallery of LOGS 2012 events in the second part of the book is the work of freelance photographer Jim Holden: www.jimholden.co.uk

The photographs of the staff were taken by Peter Whyte.

Foreword

by Norman Baker,
MP for Lewes

There are not many places that can claim an unbroken run of five hundred years, even in a town so venerable and so steeped in history as Lewes, but Lewes Old Grammar School is one. The mortar boards and canes may have gone, and the computers and photocopiers arrived, but the pupils still troop in through the ancient door and out again to join the throng of the bustling county town, just as they would have done centuries ago.

Now the school sits comfortably in a somewhat haphazard but entirely pleasing, and very Lewes, run of buildings just north of the High Street bottleneck, well grounded and at ease with itself and its place in the town. It is almost inconspicuous – it doesn't shout out its presence – but that is because it has no need to do so. It is most firmly part of the fabric of Lewes.

It is perhaps that innate self-assurance that so inspires confidence and makes it such an attractive proposition for those looking for a good education for their children. Yet even the most awesome history can only take an institution so far. Lewes Old Grammar School would not be celebrating its remarkable anniversary without meeting the basic requirements of a school, namely to acquire and keep a reputation for being educationally successful.

Today Lewes Old Grammar School has five hundred pupils enrolled, one for each year of its existence and its highest total ever. As the quincentenary milestone is reached, we can rejoice that LOGS is burning bright.

Floreat Lewys

Appreciation

*by Michael Chartier,
Mayor of Lewes and
Vice-chair of the LOGS Trustees*

It is a surprising concidence that Lewes Old Grammar School and local government in Lewes both trace their roots to the reign of Henry VIII – in the case of the school to 1512, while the earliest town records date back to 1542.

The tragic loss of many of the school's original archives denies us the ability to identify ancient areas of cooperation between the two bodies. However, common sense would suggest that many of the original high constables and headboroughs who controlled and ran the town must have been former pupils of the school. I regret that we are unable to be more precise.

Nowadays both the Grammar School and the Town Hall are among the most prominent buildings in the High Street. Both the school and the town council value the historic aspects of the buildings they own, and are fully commited to their conservation. In addition, the pupils of the school are familiar with the Town Hall, since the building is used by the school for a variety of purposes, including formal examinations.

In conclusion, it should also be recognised that both the town council and Lewes Old Grammar School are active in the local community. The pupils each year raise considerable sums of money for charity. I count it a fortunate coincidence that in this special year I have carried out the role of mayor of the town and also served as a trustee of the school.

Introduction

The biography of an institution whose history spans five hundred years must inevitably include a giddy switchback of triumphs and disasters, yet LOGS approached its quincentenary with only a rudimentary understanding of its historic dramas. Thanks in part to a shocking and inexplicable act of twentieth century vandalism (duly recounted in the text), its archives amounted to little more than a scant collection of group photographs hanging on the waiting room walls.

Chief among the few well-known facts were Agnes Morley's endowment of 1512 and another, some two hundred years later, by Mary Jenkins, but little encouragement was to be found in the assertion by T.W. Horsfield that 'the history of the school from its foundations to the beginning of the eighteenth century is involved in almost impenetrable darkness'. It was common knowledge that those endowments had been lost during the Victorian period, but why and with what consequences were questions that simply hung in the air.

In short, there were huge gaps in the LOGS story, and the creation of a cohesive narrative demanded a hungry gathering of scraps from a variety of tables – books of local and educational history, the East Sussex Record Office, the library of the Sussex Archaeological Society, copies of contemporary local newspapers and, for the recent period, the 'vox pops' of former pupils.

No school exists isolated from the world about it. Our story, as it unfolds, sets LOGS within a broader social and educational context, both local and national. It begins grandly, with Lewes the largest town in Sussex and the seat of the first, and most sumptuous, of the country's Cluniac monasteries. The grammar school sat cheek by Southover jowl with this great institution, which appointed its master, and its scholars were put through their classical paces in rigorous medieval fashion.

Fast forward to the early 18th century and we find the town a thriving centre for weald and downland farmers, its high street and riverside wharves busy with trade and commerce. The school had now moved up to St Anne's, and was supported by

the powerful Pelham family, which produced two Whig prime ministers.

Clouds were gathering, however. By the first decades of the following century Lewes was sadly diminished in importance. Agricultural depression had dried up a large source of its income, and other towns (particularly fashionable Brighton on its doorstep) had captured much of its trade and commerce. The school not only suffered from this malaise, but was presented with a more profound challenge. In short, what was it *for*? The enterprising Victorian age needed a workforce skilled in a range of practicalities, from book-keeping to engineering, rendering a proficiency in Latin and Greek a questionable expertise.

Its position would have been more secure had the grandees who served on its board of trustees kept a closer watch on its affairs. Unhappily, as inspectors from the Charity Commission discovered, their involvement was so hands-off as to be negligent, and the school had few friends to count on when it needed them.

An author writing a history at the approach of the 400th anniversary would have been hard pressed to sound an optimistic note. The headmaster was on the verge of bankruptcy and a vociferous local campaign to revivify the school's fortunes was about to collapse. A private institution without supporting funds, the school could survive only by adapting to the changing world about it, and its subsequent history shows it struggling (sometimes precariously, sometimes with dogged success) to find a place in both the local and national education environment.

Our story concerns people as much as systems and institutions. A varied cast of headmasters passes before us, by turns weak and strong, eccentric and authoritarian, short-term and long-serving. It is also, mercifully, one with a happy ending. Even the most successful of those former heads would surely be both surprised and gratified to observe today's thriving school, with (fitting for its anniversary) a roll of no fewer than 500 pupils, the largest ever recorded in its long and compelling history.

Floreat Lewys!

David Arscott
Lewes, 2012

Part One

THE HISTORY

The Southover Years

IN MAY 1512 a wealthy, childless widow whose treasured belongings included a coconut cup (highly fashionable at the time), silver spoons adorned with acorn heads and rosaries with beads of coral and gold, bequeathed land and money for the establishment of a 'free school' in Southover.

Agnes Morley's rather long-winded will left little to chance. The master of her new foundation was to be a priest, but one free of any distracting ecclesiastical responsibilities. Under him there would be an usher, and both would be appointed by the prior of the great monastic pile next door.

Although he must concentrate on the teaching of grammar, the schoolmaster-priest did have one other important job to do. Agnes was to be buried in St John's church, and it would be his duty to pray regularly in the chapel of St Erasmus, the patron

Facing page: The ruins of St Pancras Priory, with the tower of St John's church behind. In the early 16th century it was one of the great religious houses of England.

Below: A copy of Agnes Morley's will. The prior was to choose the headmaster of her new school, and prayers were to be said for her soul in St John's church. [ESRO]

In Dei Domine Amen This is the last Will of me Agnes Morley Widowe of the Parish of Saint John Baptist of Southover next to Lewes in the County of Sussex made the 24th day of the Month of May in Year of our Lord 1512 and in the 4th year of the Reigne of King Henry the 8th as concerning the establishing and ordering a Free School in Southover aforesaid perpetually tobe continued in manner and form following that is to say Whereas I the aforesaid Agnes late purchased jointly with others tobe our Heirs and Assigns of Edmund Dudley an annual rent or annuity of £20 by the year tobe received and taken of and in his Mannor of Hammesley otherwise Hammes next to Lewes in the County of Sussex with a proviso as in Certa Significata et Sigillat Manibus ipius Edmundi Cujus Dat est decimo Sexto die mensis Decembris anno Regni Regis Henrici Septimi Vicesimo Tertio plenius Apparet And also where diverse persons be seased of and in a Messuage and a Garden in Southover aforesaid lying next to the Mill called Watergate to my use and performance of this my last Will Imprimis I will that said Messuage and garden with the Apptce shall serve for a School master and an Usher there to dwell in to teach Grammar in the same for ever Itm I will

13

1509–47
Reign of Henry VIII

1512
Free Grammar School founded in Southover

1517
Martin Luther's 95 theses prompt rise of Protestantism

1536–40
Dissolution of the monasteries

1537
Southover Priory is the first religious house in England to surrender to the Crown

1538
Lewes Greyfriars friary confiscated 'to the king's use'

1542
First mention of the 'Twelve' governing Lewes

1545
Suppression of college of canons at Malling

Right: The position of the original school in what is now Grange Gardens, based on Agnes Morley's will and recent OS maps. Although Southover Grange is believed to date from 1572, there may have been an earlier building on the site. [John Houghton]

saint of sick children, both for her soul and for the 'feoffees' (or trustees) she had entrusted with safegarding the school's assets. Part of her endowment was to finance the upkeep of the chapel and pay for wine, wax and 'other things necessary for a priest to sing with'.

Agnes Morley wanted no fly-by-nights running her school. The master had to give a full year's notice when he wanted to leave, and the usher six months. Indeed, so determined was she that her educational dream should be realised that she included a threat to her four young nephews in her testament. They were all set to receive legacies when she died, but they would get nothing unless they disclaimed any right to the school property. And if they refused? In that case she ordered that their legacies be withheld and 'the same money and plate to bee putte into my cheste whiche belongith and ys ordeyned for the saide Free Scole, and there to remayne to the use and performation of the forsaide Free Scole'.

Its premises were a house and garden 'lying next to the mylle called Watergate', and here the school would remain for a full two hundred years. Although nothing survives, we know that it stood in the south-east corner of today's Grange Gardens, between Eastport Lane and the Winterbourne stream. The millpond lay in a hollow subject to heavy flooding during the calamitous inundations of 1960 and 2000.

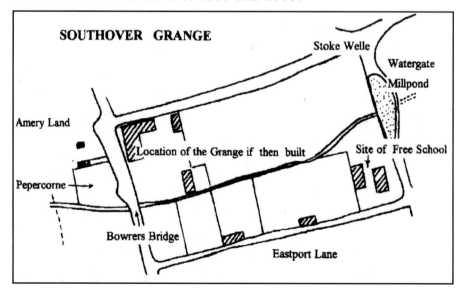

A CLOSE CALL

Academics have argued over whether the word 'free' in the title originally referred to an education without fees or to a school's independence from the church. This became a crucial issue after Henry VIII's agents set about plundering and destroying the religious houses in the 1530s, with Agnes Morley's school in real danger of being obliterated in its infancy.

The dissolution of the monasteries followed hard on the heels of Henry's feud with the Pope over his divorce from Catherine of Aragon. Its speed and comprehensiveness is epitomised by the brutal slighting of the great Priory of St Pancras at Southover. William de Warenne, the Norman lord who ruled Lewes after the Conquest, founded it with his wife Gundrada soon after they visited Burgundy in 1075. The first Cluniac monastery in England, it became immensely rich and influential. It's known to have founded no fewer than three grammar schools (at Melton Mowbray and Halifax as well as Southover) and owned vast stretches of land the length and breadth of the kingdom. Its church was more magnificent than Chichester Cathedral – and yet it was to disappear almost in an instant, leaving scarcely a trace of its glories behind.

In October 1535 the State inquisitor Richard Layton arrived at Southover intent on uncovering corruption. He reported to Henry's feared minister Thomas Cromwell that he had accused the prior, Robert Crowham, of being 'a heinous traitor with the worst words I could deliver, he all the time kneeling, making intercession unto me not to utter to you the premises of his undoing'. Not surprisingly, Crowham and his 22 monks decided to surrender the priory and its assets 'with unanimous assent'.

Cromwell sent the Italian military engineer Giovanni Portinari to demolish the buildings. In 1538 he came with a team of 17 men, melting the lead on the roofs and undermining the walls by setting fire to huge wooden staves which had been driven into the ground beneath them.

Crowham had clearly foreseen difficulties for the school, because in 1536 he arranged for fourteen new trustees to be appointed, most of them members of the local gentry. It seems likely that he wished to protect the school from being seen as

---

EARLY LEARNING

Lewes Priory ran a school in Southover long before Agnes Morley's time, and hers may even have been a continuation of it.

The earliest known reference is in 1248, when the local monks chose their 'beloved clerk Lucas, schoolmaster of Lewes', to represent them in a legal case held before the papal auditor in Rome.

The priory objected to paying tithes to the 'mother abbey' in Cluny, but after a number of hearings punctuated by delays Lucas eventually admitted defeat.

In 1285 Archbishop Peckham wrote to the abbot of Cluny, saying that Lewes Priory was dearer to him than any other house in England – and seeming to imply that he was himself educated in Lewes.

Later that year John de Hampton, master of Lewes School, was ordained at South Malling.

A further mention occurs in 1405, when the will of John Wodewey includes the line: 'I owe the schoolmaster of Lewes 6d.'

1545

Sir Nicholas Pelham defeats French raiders: his memorial in St Michael's church (below) records that 'What time ye French sought to have sackt Sea-foord/ This Pelham did repell them back aboord'

1547–53

Reign of Edward VI

1547

Sherman's chantry chapel confiscated

The former church of St Peter Westout, which housed Sherman's Chantry

simply an adjunct of the priory, which had fallen so dramatically out of favour. It was further imperilled by the stipulation in Agnes Morley's will that masses should be said for her soul in St John's church. Chantries, as these arrangements were called, were now regarded as a Romish superstition. First Henry appropriated their funds and the lands which provided their income, and then, in 1547, his successor, Edward VI, issued an act suppressing more than two thousand of them. The closure of Sherman's chantry chapel in Lewes would later (*page 26*) become part of our story.

When the Crown agent Anthony Stringer visited Southover, probably in that same year, he found the school without a master, but the fact that it was still running (under an usher) reveals that it had survived its initial crisis. It was a feature of Edward's reign for chantry priests to become teachers in grammar schools funded by the reassigned income, and Stringer now approved the general state of affairs at Southover, reporting a healthy annual revenue and the lodging of a substantial deposit in the school chest.

As to the subject of the master, he noted that Lewes was a populous town with 'much youth', and that the locals wanted a learned man to fill the post. He went so far as to suggest Thomas Otley, the parson of Ripe and a former lecturer in logic and Greek at Oxford, but Otley instead took himself off to become vicar of Burwash.

LATIN, GREEK – AND A GOOD THRASHING

What was it like to be a pupil in a late medieval grammar school? The boys – and *only* boys, of course – underwent the same rigorous training wherever they were. Reading and writing was taken care of in elementary school: once lads went into grammar school, at some time between the ages of eight and 11, Latin was the mainstay of their education. There was no science, no English history, no English literature. There may have been some arithmetic, often paid for as an extra, and some instruction in the Christian faith, but there was little else that most of today's schoolchildren would recognise. It was six days a week, and heaven help you if you didn't pay attention to the sermon on

Sundays, because a Monday morning question-and-answer session ('catechising') on what the priest had said was common in an era when you were fined for not going to church. Fridays were usually spent revising what had been done earlier in the week, and some kindly establishments allowed a half-holiday on Thursdays, known – rather aptly – as a 'remedy'.

The day started early (six o'clock in the summer and seven in the winter), and it was long, finishing around half-past five or six o'clock, with a lunch break at eleven, when most boys would have scrambled home for something to sustain them through a long afternoon. Those hours were tough, because they were filled with drilling and repetition, with rote learning and textual analysis, and with the ever-present encouragement of the birch. The teaching technique demanded strictness, not charisma or originality, and those who entered the profession were expected to make their mark on the backsides of their pupils. A candidate for the final examination in grammar at Cambridge University was expected to prove he was up to teaching by flogging a boy – under exam conditions, as it were.

A grammar school education usually lasted six or seven years. Although it wasn't for the faint-hearted, this system produced – or at least failed to extinguish – the genius of William Shakespeare, as well as his fellow playwright Christopher Marlowe, the poet

Teaching in a medieval grammar school, as depicted in an illustrated manuscript. [British Library]

Capital from the priory at Southover

A vigorous flogging in a medieval school, carved on a misericord in Sherborne Abbey, Dorset.

1553–58
Reign of Queen Mary

1555–57
Seventeen Protestant martyrs burned at Lewes

Plaque outside Lewes Town Hall, formerly the Star Inn

The martyrs' memorial above Cliffe

John Milton, Lord Chancellor Thomas More, physicist Isaac Newton and architect Christopher Wren, to name only a few.

Most grammar school boys were from prosperous local families. (Lads who were to spend their lives walking behind a plough or bent over a blacksmith's anvil needed no appreciation of a well-rounded Ciceronian sentence or a poignant line from Euripides.) Latin was thought to be the right study for a gentleman in the making, for those born at the top and for those somewhat lower down who aspired to put their *sons* at the top. The Reformation also brought the revival of ancient Greek, hitherto almost lost in England, another language full of complexity and traps for the young scholars down by the stream in Southover, or at least for those in the higher forms and those bound for one of the two universities.

Schools such as Lewes were following a pattern formalised in much larger establishments, including Eton, Winchester and St Paul's in London. The grammar books or primers written for those schools, and the classical texts studied there, were copied throughout England. It was a pattern that would last, with a few additions, for centuries.

The boys would have been taught in a single large room by one or two masters – usually a headmaster and an assistant, or usher. They had to provide their own pens, paper and candles and sat on forms, ranked according to ability rather than age, while the master sat at the front on a chair, possibly with a sounding board above his head, like an old-fashioned pulpit, so that his voice would carry. Recitation and repetition wouldn't have made for a silent schoolroom, and the boys were taught to dispute in Latin as well as to write it. In fact learning was largely oral – one of the aims was to teach the art of oratory – and until the mid- to late-sixteenth century books would have been very few. It's quite possible that, as was the case in many English grammar schools of the time, the Southover boys had to speak Latin throughout the day.

Rigorous and physically painful though their Tudor schoolroom undoubtedly was, however, to many of them it must have appeared a safe and stable haven compared with the torments of life outside.

BLOODY QUEEN MARY

In July 1553 the Roman Catholic Mary Tudor came to the throne and, overnight, the religious and political life of the country was turned on its head. Lewes and the surrounding area had for long been a hotbed of protestantism, and seventeen brave and unbending men and women were burned to death for their faith outside the Star Inn – on the site of the present town hall.

It's scarcely possible to put ourselves in the shoes of a sensitive lad conscious of such brutality being played out a few hundred yards up the hill from his schoolroom. Perhaps he stuffed his ears and managed to blot it out of his mind. It would have been impossible, though, to be unaware of the day-to-day changes as fervent Catholics seized the opportunity to turn back the clock.

For one thing the religious teaching in the classroom would have swiftly reverted to its pre-Protestant form. The headmaster during Mary's reign was Gabriel Fowle, and in his will he asked for ten priests 'if they can be got' to celebrate masses for his soul. Yes, chantries were back with a vengeance, and doubtless the soul of Agnes Morley was once again 'sung' for in St John's.

Mary was determined to police the nation's schools, keeping their finances under tight control and subjecting their masters to examination and licensing by bishops or other senior churchmen – a system which would continue for some long time after her reign. Graduates of Oxford and Cambridge were desirable, and it was all the better if they had been ordained.

The Southover school passed the test. The trustees had dipped into their own pockets to increase the school funds, and their so-called 'chief doer', John Stempe, whose father had been an official at the priory, persuaded the Treasury that its assets were in good shape, that the buildings had been repaired and that (a question of settled scores, presumably) the master and usher had been reimbursed for 'meat and drink' previously available at the priory.

One of the school's trustees, Edward Gage of Firle, was a vicious persecutor of Protestants. As high sheriff he had thirteen 'heretics' burned to death, and when John Trewe of Hellingly 'persuaded the people from going to mass' Gage had his ears cropped and set him in the Lewes pillory.

Priory seal, 1343

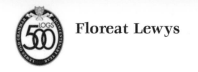

1558–1603
Reign of Elizabeth I

1564–1616
Life of William Shakespeare

1572
*William Newton builds
Southover Grange, using stone
from the dismantled priory*

*Carving of a monk's face in
Grange Gardens*

1587
Mary Queen of Scots executed

1588
*Elizabeth sends 42 barrels of
gunpowder to Lewes ahead of
a threatened Spanish invasion.
The Armada sails along the
Sussex coast in late July, and
is soon defeated*

ELIZABETHAN ORDER

Since Mary's reign was short, it's not inconceivable that some rather perplexed students may have witnessed two abrupt changes in religious instruction during their time at the school. When her half-sister Elizabeth became queen, Protestant worship was re-instated, with priests (and priest-schoolmasters) once more jumping on and off the clerical roundabout.

By the second half of the sixteenth century, priests were allowed to be married. Many combined their clerical work with teaching, living in a school with a wife and family, and augmenting their income by offering boarding to boys who lived at some distance. This perk was to be a feature of our grammar school for centuries to come, despite Agnes Morley stipulating that the master should have no 'cure of soule'.

Under Elizabeth there were far few executions than in Mary's time, although some Roman Catholics did pay the ultimate price for their faith or their political activities. These included Thomas Howard, the first Duke of Norfolk to have Arundel connections and, even nearer home, Edward Shelley of Bentley, found guilty of harbouring a Catholic priest.

The Elizabethan age saw the rise of a new land-owning gentry. Many of these 'new men' had profited from the dispersal of monastic possessions after the Dissolution. They now built themselves handsome mansions of solid stone and warm brick, and were soon indispensable pillars of their communities as justices of the peace, magistrates and members of Parliament.

Students of the free school during the 1570s watched one such pile rise up before their eyes across the Winterbourne stream. William Newton used stone from the ruined priory to create the building we now know as the Grange. It would later be the home of the school's most famous pupil, John Evelyn. Newton's initials and the date *1572* are carved (*below*) on one of the fireplaces.

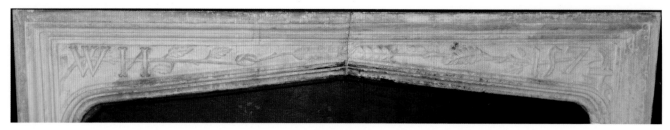

JOHN EVELYN, *diarist*

As his epitaph reminds us, John Evelyn lived in 'an age of extraordinary events and revolutions', and his celebrated diaries document the deaths of Charles I and Oliver Cromwell (both of which he witnessed), the last great plague of London and the Great Fire of London in 1666.

As a five-year-old he came to Sussex in 1625 to live with his maternal grandparents, the Stansfields. 'This was the year,' he later recorded, 'in which the pestilence was so epidemical that there dy'd in London 5,000 a week.'

The young Evelyn laid a foundation stone at South Malling church when it was rebuilt in 1627 (his grandfather had paid for much of the work). He first went to a school in the Cliffe, but after his widowed grandmother had married William Newton, son of the man who built the Grange, Evelyn went to live with them there, enrolling at the grammar school under Edward Snatt.

Although he would later go up to Balliol College, Oxford, he was by his own account a lazy student 'extremely remiss in my studies'. His father, thought him spoiled by his grandmother and wanted to send him to Eton, but 'unreasonably terrified with the report of the severe discipline there, I was sent back to Lewes, which perversenesse of mine I have since a thousand times deplored'.

Perhaps he exaggerated his slothfulness and the time he had wasted in 'drawing and designing'. At any rate he later enjoyed a stellar career, both as an horticulturist and an author on a wide variety of subjects. He was also a member of the group that founded the Royal Society and, during the Second Anglo-Dutch War, served as a commissioner for the care of sick and wounded seamen and for the care and treatment of prisoners of war.

His vast library comprised 3,859 books and 822 pamphlets, many of them bound 'in the French taste' and bearing his motto *Omnia explorate; meliora retinete* – Explore everything; keep the better.

Southover Grange, where the young John Evelyn came to live when his grandmother married William Newton.

1603–1625
Reign of James I (James VI of Scotland)

1605
Gunpowder Plot

1611
Thomas Blunt's bequests to the town and the grammar school

The silver bowl Thomas Blunt gave to the town in 1611

HERBERT MORLEY, *politician*

A Puritan politician in dangerous times, Morley (no close relation of the school's founder, Agnes) hailed from Glynde and spent the Civil War as a roundhead colonel raising troops in Sussex. When royalist forces took Arundel and Chichester he helped General Waller recapture them for Parliament.

He was returned as an MP in the three Protectorate Parliaments during the 1650s, and again in the Convention Parliament of 1660.

Although nominated a judge for the trial of Charles I, Morley refused to sign his death warrant. This saved his life and enabled him to purchase a pardon (for a very large sum) when Charles II came to the throne in 1660.

He was re-elected MP for Rye in 1661 in the Cavalier Parliament, and sat until his death six years later.

Glynde Place, the home of Herbert Morley and, later, a governor of the free school, Viscount Hampden.

BLUNT'S BOUNTY

The school celebrated its first century with a new endowment in place. Thomas Blunt, a barber-surgeon, was one of the Twelve, the caucus of the Lewes great and good who, along with the constables, looked after the town's affairs. He died in 1611, leaving his colleagues a double-gilt silver bowl as 'a pledge of his love'. In addition he directed his trustees to donate portions of the rent from his house in Lewes (now 171–172 High Street) to six local parishes and – a small but useful sum – to the headmasters of the free school in Southover in perpetuity.

The school was in good heart during the seventeenth century, and it's pleasing to imagine four young lads who would all later make names for themselves crossing the bridge by the mill at Watergate to sit side by side in the classroom of the wonderfully named Edward Snatt – the puritan MP and Roundhead colonel Herbert Morley (1616–1667), the diarist and horticulturist John Evelyn (1620–1706), the renowned herbalist Nicholas Culpeper (1616–1654), and the printer, political writer and Roundhead quartermaster-general John Streater (1620–1677). The first two were without doubt pupils at the grammar school, the latter two almost certainly so.

Snatt's son William would later become a persecutor of the local Quakers, but the headmaster himself seems to have been a benign influence, and Evelyn continued to keep in touch with him in later life. 'Perhaps,' Colin Brent surmises, 'Snatt was unusually indulgent to a boy whose father served as sheriff of Sussex and Surrey in 1633, attended by 116 retainers clad in doublets of green satin.' Evelyn sent him copies of his writings.

Some of the illustrations in John Evelyn's unpublished Elysium Brittanicum *were drawn when he was a pupil at the grammar school, and depict garden equipment then in use at the Grange.* [British Library]

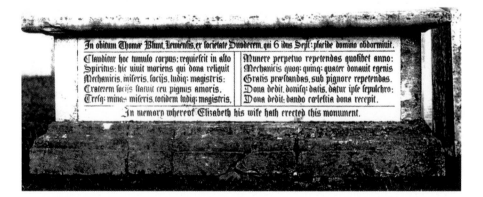

Thomas Blunt's tomb in the churchyard of St John sub Castro with a list, in Latin, of all his bequests. Today the lettering is weather-worn and covered with ivy.

1625–49
Reign of Charles I

1642–1651
English Civil War

1649
Charles I executed; England declared a Commonwealth

A MERCIFUL DEATH

Several Sussex men were among the 59 judges (or commissioners) who signed the death warrant of Charles I. All were at risk of a terrible revenge should events turn against them – as later they did.

Some of the regicides fled abroad, where they were pursued by agents of the restored Charles II. Others were imprisoned, while several were executed under the Indemnity and Oblivion Act of 1660 – some being gruesomely hanged, drawn and quartered.

The Lewes MP Anthony Stapley, who would certainly have been a hunted man, had the fortune to die a natural death in 1655.

John Streater, *soldier & pamphleteer*

A formidable figure in the tempestuous years of the Civil War, Streater was a successful soldier and a controversial publisher of political pamphlets.

He was brought up in Lewes, his father having a master tailor's business in the high street between St Michael's church and Pipe Passage. In 1635, at the age of 15, he was apprenticed to a London stationer, and he would later become a printer and publisher in his own right.

Like both Herbert Morley and Nicholas Culpeper, he fought for Parliament's cause against the king, and by the early 1650s he was quartermaster-general of the forces which conquered Catholic Ireland. He was always very much his own man, however, and he was vigorously opposed to what he saw as monarchical tendencies in Cromwell's dominance over parliament. He argued instead for a republic of energetic citizens who would elect MPs and officials for fixed terms and would subject them to laws written in basic English – so protecting ordinary people from the tyranny of lawyers.

Painting by Dom Ramos

Imprisoned in 1653 for writing an article entitled 'The grand politick informer', he later learned to produce pamphlets which expressed his anti-government views in a more subtle fashion.

After the Restoration his presses continued to roll, one of his publications being *The London Dispensory* by his old friend Culpeper. He was in trouble again in 1670 for writing a seditious libel, but he survived to make a further military impact – inventing a new kind of 'fire-shot' or grenade at the time of the second Anglo-Dutch war.

His end was less happy. He died a prisoner in the infamous London debtors' gaol, the Marshalsea.

'This is the third book that I have received from your Honour,' Snatt wrote gushingly on receiving his translation of Lucretius in 1657. 'The third book, I say, of your own making, which makes me stand amazed; I cannot tell whether more at the excellency of your work in writing, or at your condescension so low as to stoop to give it me in such a manner.' The roles of master and pupil seem almost to have been reversed.

Not even the bitter rivalries of the Civil War (mercifully the last internecine blood-letting on our shores) seem to have had a huge impact on the ability of the school to continue producing able scholars. The register of St John's College, Cambridge, reveals that in April 1646 Edward Beecher, a Lewes tailor's son, was admitted there as a sizar – an undergraduate receiving financial help from the university and expected to perform various menial duties in return. He had been 'bred under Mr Golding', who was presumably the grammar school headmaster at the time.

Several Lewes pupils made the pilgrimage to St John's over the years. Timothy, the son of 'Thomas Burrell, gentleman, of Cuckfield' went there in 1682 (his headmaster was Thomas Whalley, William Snatt's brother-in-law), as in 1700 did Thomas Denham of Withyham, who had been taught by a Mr Reading. That connection between the grammar school and the great universities was to continue for decades to come.

STEERE'S CHARITY

In 1661 Rev George Steere willed the income derived from the rents and profits of his houses in the town (one at 76 High Street and three on the west side of Market Lane) to 'the education and maintenance of one fit person, the son of godly poor parents, in or near the said town of Lewes, especially the son of a godly poor minister who hath truly laboured and endeavoured to win souls unto Jesus Christ, at one of the Universities of Cambridge or Oxford'.

The charity had no direct connection with the grammar school, but some of its headmasters made use of it for their own sons. As one of their number, Robert Austen, wrote in a letter, it was a perk 'easily to be obtained'.

The monument in All Saints church to John Evelyn's grandparents. John Stansfield played a major role in the rebuilding of South Malling church, and the young Evelyn laid one of the foundation stones.

1651
'Great Escape' of future Charles II through Sussex

1660–85
Reign of Charles II

1660
'New building' at the school

1678
Titus Oates' 'Popish Plot'

1685–59
Reign of James II

1689
'The Glorious Revolution': William & Mary called to the throne

1689–1694
Reign of William III and Mary

1694–1702
(Death of Queen Mary) Reign of William III

1702–1714
Reign of Queen Anne

1709
Mary Jenkins' gift to the grammar school

Lewes had been solidly Puritan during the conflict which culminated in the beheading of the king, and it remained so after the Restoration of 1660, when Charles II returned to England to claim the throne. Within a year all members of the Twelve were debarred from civic office by an unforgiving royalist government, and when the Anglican state church was also restored many locals became Dissenters, refusing to attend services and suffering punishments in consequence.

In these circumstances it's surely significant that in May 1660 – the very month that Charles returned in triumph – Walter Brett was authorised to spend county funds on what was described as 'the new building of the free school'. This suggests at the least an expansion of the premises if not a complete reconstruction, and it's tempting to imagine a new board of trustees emerging from a power struggle and determined to remake the school in their own image.

ENTER MARY JENKINS

No conjecture is required to tell the next part of the story. In 1709 Mrs Mary Jenkins gave in trust for the master of the free school in Southover 'a messuage or tenement, stable, garden and appurtenances situated in the parish of St Peter & St Mary Westout, and formerly the Chauntry house'.

That house – on the site of today's grammar school – was one of various properties which had provided the income to support Sherman's chantry in St Peter's church on the other side of the road. As we've seen (*page 16*), the chantry was confiscated by Edward VI. The chantry house and the land around it (probably including what is now the Shelleys car park) had been sold by the Crown into private hands as early as 1549. Mrs Jenkins, born in Alciston but living in London, bought it the year before she gave it away.

Her gift was a major one, including a large pot of money as well as the substantial house provided for the enjoyment of the headmaster. The figures are in themselves meaningless today, but they stand comparison: Agnes Morley had left £10 a year to the master and £5 to his usher; Thomas Blunt's bequest of 1611 yielded £3 to the master; and now Mary Jenkins' capital allowed

NICHOLAS CULPEPER *Herbalist*

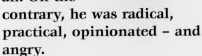

A man who practised as a herbalist, physician and astrologer might be imagined as gentle and unworldly, but that wasn't Nicholas Culpeper's character at all. On the contrary, he was radical, practical, opinionated – and angry.

Brought up at Isfield, he spent most of his time in the outdoors, learning the lore of plants at first hand. His published works include *The English Physician* (1652), the *Complete Herbal* (1653) and *Astrological Judgement of Diseases from the Decumbiture of the Sick* (1655). The first two are still read today, while the third is regarded as one of the most detailed documents on the practice of medical astrology in Early Modern Europe.

He set up a pharmacy in London and – arguing that no man deserved to starve in order to pay 'an insulting, insolent physician' – would see as many as forty people in a morning, charging nothing for his services.

(He had married a wealthy merchant's daughter and obtained his herbal supplies from the countryside nearby.) He wrote his books in English, rather than Latin, so that the ordinary man and woman could benefit from them.

The son of a clergyman, Culpeper was an ardent Puritan. At the beginning of the Civil War he was accused of witchcraft, and the Society of Apothecaries tried to stop him practising. In 1643 he joined a Parliamentary train-band (a company of trained militia) and fought at the first battle of Newbury, carrying out battlefield surgery along the way.

He sustained a serious chest wound in the fighting, from which he never fully recovered. Returning home, he collaborated with the Republican astrologer William Lilly to write a prediction of the king's death entitled *A Prophesy of the White King*.

What revenge would have been meted out to him at the Restoration we can only guess: Culpeper died of tuberculosis in January 1654 at the age of 38.

Still popular after all these years: top, the original Complete Herbal *of 1653; above, a modern reprint.*

1714–27

Reign of George I

c. 1714

Lewes Free School moves from Southover to its present site in St Anne's parish

1726

The wooden bridge over the Ouse at Cliffe is washed away by heavy floods

1727

A new bridge opens, designed in brick and stone by Nicholas Dubois

The new Lewes Bridge

for the spending of up to £15 a year on books, with the rest earmarked for the staff – a nest-egg which in 1775 gave the master £20 10s and a writing master £17 15s.

The man who first enjoyed this largesse and carried the school forward confidently into its third century was Thomas Peirce, who had been the headmaster since 1706. He now had a commodious new house – and would soon be taking the boys with him.

Thomas Peirce's name appears alongside the date 1718 on the list of rectors at St Thomas church in the Cliffe. Other grammar school heads represented are Thomas Whalley (1690) and Evan Griffiths (1932).

Up the Hill to St Anne's

THE CREAKING LEGS of old Thomas Peirce were, it seems, one reason why the school moved from Southover to its new home outside the old west gate of Lewes. Within a few years of the Jenkins gift the trustees sanctioned the building of a new schoolroom on the St Anne's site, and the headmaster now had only a step to take from his living quarters to the classroom.

That laboured climb up cobbled Keere Street every evening had not only left him gasping for breath, but transported him from one distinct administrative area to another – Southover (like Cliffe) would merge into a common borough with Lewes only in 1881, and complaints would later be heard from families down the hill that they were being cold-shouldered by 'their' grammar school at its new headquarters up in the town.

The size of the building enabled Peirce and future masters to take in large numbers of fee-paying boarders, and the obvious temptation was to expand their number at the expense of the free boys. This would certainly become a contentious issue in the years to come, but Peirce himself seems to have drawn no criticism on this count. Rather, the very liveliness of his full

The house given by Mary Jenkins for the headmaster's use became the home of the grammar school itself from around 1714 (the trustees released the necessary cash a year later), and LOGS still occupies the site today. This pencil sketch was drawn by John Buckler in 1830, some twenty years before the school was rebuilt. [British Library]

1727–60
Reign of George II

1743–54
Henry Pelham prime minister

1754–1756
Duke of Newcastle prime minister

1757–1762
Henry Pelham prime minister

The Pelham buckle

DOWN MEMORY LANE

Thomas Peirce obviously retained a strong affection for his old schoolhouse by the Grange.

Although he found the journey arduous, once a year he would take all his pupils down the hill to the echoing and decaying building and put them through their lessons as in days of yore.

house was singled out for praise by the Society for Promoting Christian Knowledge (SPCK), which observed that the school 'flourishes under his conduct' and added that 'the Sons of Considerable Gentlemen boarding with him in ye Town gives him an opportunity of an Enlarged Conversation by which he may be useful to promote ye designs of ye Society'.

What Peirce *was* criticised for was spending too much time on his clerical duties – as a curate at St Anne's and then rector of St Thomas's. He found the boys 'very often dull, and too often incorrigible'. Josiah Welby, who followed him in 1725, was obliged by the trustees to promise not to take holy orders, since 'my predecessor was negligent in his teaching school, because he had his hands full in the cure of his parishes'.

Welby broke his promise shortly before the end of his 20-year stint at the school, and Mrs Morley's stipulation, and the trustees' initial resolve in enforcing it, seem to have been forgotten in the years that followed.

LIVELY LEWES

The school's fortunes have generally swung up and down to match the prosperity or otherwise of its host town, and the early Georgian era was a time of growth. In the preceding years, the historian Colin Brent has written, 'Lewes had played several parts, as a hub of commerce, of decentralised government, of intellectual debate, and by 1714 its emergence as a county town was complete'.

In *Georgian Lewes 1714–1830* he gives a vivid pen-portrait of a thriving community based on agriculture:

> After the grammar school and the west gate, on a level stretch, came the Presbyterian meeting house and St Michael's church, where sat the archdeacon's court; then the market house with its whipping post, clock and proclamations board, and the Town Hall which housed the quarter sessions and assizes; here too clustered the wholesale vintners, grocers and drapers, the goldsmiths and gunsmiths, and two commodious hostelries, the White Hart and the Star; beyond the clock house School Hill plunged past the consulting rooms of wealthy lawyers and physicians down to the town wharf and the bridge.

Boys from well-to-do backgrounds who lodged at the grammar school mixed their classical learning with developing their social graces, as exemplified by young Nicholas Gilbert from Eastbourne. He came to Lewes at Michaelmas term 1714 at the age of seven, his lawyer father having died the year before, and he boarded there for the next five years.

His guardians kept a record of the money spent on him. Apart from Peirce's fees, separate amounts were paid to writing and dancing masters, a draper and a shoemaker, and Nicholas also had his head shaved regularly so that he could wear a wig – the mark of a private pupil as opposed to a free scholar.

WHIGS *v* TORIES

Compared with the turmoil of the previous centuries, Georgian England was, politically and religiously, calm, ordered and settled. A small minority had the vote, but the country was a functioning democracy, with rule through parliament. The two main political groups, the boisterously opposed Whigs and Tories, would later evolve into the Liberal and Conservative parties we know today.

Lewes had long been known for its large contingent of dissenters and independents, and most of these flocked to the Whig banner, led by the powerful Pelham family and their associates, such as the Shelleys. Their buckle emblem can be seen on several buildings in the Lewes area, but their influence wasn't merely local: under George II, both Henry Pelham (twice) and his brother, the Duke of Newcastle – a champion of the grammar school – served as British prime ministers.

Henry Pelham (top) and his brother, the Duke of Newcastle. The duke was a supporter of the grammar school – and his Tory opponents took their revenge on it. [British Library]

Pelham House, the family's Lewes base during the 18th century.

1760–1820
Reign of George III

1768–74
Thomas Paine lives in Lewes and writes his first pamphlet

Thomas Paine

1775–1782
American War of Independence

1789
Start of French Revolution

DUNVAN'S LEWES

In 1795 Paul Dunvan, a former assistant master at the grammar school, published his *Ancient and Modern History of Lewes and Brighthelmston*.

He suggests that the millpond by the old school by the Grange was 'the place where William de Witton, one of Henry the Third's justiciaries, was drowned in his flight from the battle of Lewes'.

The trustees of the Jenkins bequest were Whig supporters, but the interference of the Pelhams in the school's affairs wasn't always benign. For one thing education became part of the bribery culture of the day: Josiah Welby and a later headmaster, Robert Austen, had to oblige the duke by enrolling the sons of his cronies among the free boys. For another, the Tories were provoked into retaliation: during one election Welby was horrified to find them poaching his boarders and thereby threatening his precarious livelihood.

COMPETITION

One lad given a free place his father could doubtless afford was a son of the Verrall family at the White Hart inn. His father told the duke that the boy had become 'a great Proficient' in Latin, arithmetic and writing, and was now fit for a clerk's post in 'The Treasury, Customs, War, Pay or Stamp Office'.

A problem for the grammar school was that although it probably led the way in Latin, a host of other academies had sprung up offering courses useful to a spreading commercial class. Young Verrall had his tuition for nothing, but the parents of other lads must have looked carefully at what was on offer across the board, and how the fees compared.

William Gwynne, who was the headmaster from 1778 until 1807, evidently felt the impact of his competition. In January 1779 he was offering 'the Greek and Latin Classics' for £25 a year, but four months later this had been reduced to £21. Two years later he seemed to have compromised regarding the curriculum:

> Though the Knowledge of the GREEK and LATIN Classics is professedly the more immediate Object of Pursuit in the above School; yet particular Care is taken that the Scholars read the ENGLISH Language with Taste and write it with Accuracy and Elegance.

Later that same year there were further additions:

> In the above SCHOOL are taught the Greek, Latin and English Languages; Writing and Arithmetic. After this Recess will be taught also French and Geography.

RICHARD RUSSELL *Doctor*

He didn't actually create Brighton, as some have claimed, but Richard Russell – a son of Lewes, and a pupil at the grammar school – was certainly a major figure in its rapid expansion during the late 18th and early 19th centuries.

As the author of the treatise *A Dissertation on the Use of Sea Water in the Affections of the Glands* (written in Latin before an English version came out in 1752), he championed the so-called 'sea water cure' – drinking it as well as swimming in it – which was all the rage at seaside resorts up and down the land.

He first practised in Lewes (there's a plaque on the building, across the road from the castle), but much more money was to be made in Brighton, which was already outstripping Lewes in size and reputation.

He had a house cum consulting rooms fashioned for himself on the seafront, where the Royal Albion Hotel now stands. A plaque, echoing Christopher Wren's at St Paul's, reads 'If you seek his monument, look around'.

Russell was buried back in his home town. There's another fitting tribute on his memorial in the church at South Malling, this time from the Greek of Euripides: it translates as 'The sea washes away all the ills of mankind'.

DR. RICHARD RUSSELL F.R.S. (1687-1759) AUTHOR OF A DISSERTATION CONCERNING THE USE OF SEA WATER IN DISEASES OF THE GLANDS (1750). FOUNDER OF BRIGHTON AS A BATHING RESORT. BORN AND PRACTISED MEDICINE IN THIS HOUSE. 1988

A LITTLE BIT EXTRA

Apart from their income from the school's various endowments and from taking boarders, masters also enjoyed 'tips' from satisfied parents.

The long-serving Robert Austen (head from 1748 until 1775) taught the sons of the Lewes surgeon-apothecary Henry Manning. At a time when the annual fee was two guineas, plus extras, Manning twice slipped a further two guineas to Austen as a 'perquisite', with a further 10s 6d going to the usher.

1805
Battle of Trafalgar

1806
Town Act establishes improvement commisioners to pave, light, cleanse, watch and repair the roads and other public places in Lewes

1815
Battle of Waterloo; George, the Prince Regent, begins his Royal Pavilion

Gwynne was apparently popular with his pupils, who on one occasion lavished praise on him in song as 'a master that ne'er lived to plague us', but he played fast and loose with the 'free school' rules. His predecessor, Robert Austen, reporting his income to the trustees, had acknowledged the use of a 'commodious house for the purpose of taking boarders with a Stable and Garden' and added that for the salary from the Jenkins charity he was supposed to teach '12 to 20' boys.

He himself had about a dozen on the register, a figure which came to be regarded as the desirable number. Gwynne, although he had thirty people living in his house in 1790, had at most six 'foundation' places filled at that time, and later reports suggest that he had run the number of free boys down to zero by the time he resigned in 1807.

Who was he teaching? Some genteel but hand-to-mouth widows were attracted to the town in the hope of finding a free place for their sons in a school with a lingering reputation, but most of his pupils were now from the professional classes. 'Socially,' Brent notes, 'the bottom-line was drawn below surveyors and master printers.'

Farewell to the old school

Agnes Morley's original school by the mill in Southover decayed year by year after the move to St Anne's, and in 1808 Colonel Newton at the Grange bought the building and the land on which it stood in order to increase the size of his 'pleasure ground'.

He presumably had it demolished at once. A later report by the Charity Commissioners referred to its having been used as a barrel-makers warehouse and then as a 'smith's shop', but John Hoper, who helped strike the deal with Newton, described its state in 1808 as 'merely a tinker's workshop, with a small garden and totally useless for the purpose for which it was intended'.

Newton generously paid £300 for the property against a valuation of £250, and the proceeds were invested in government bonds to swell the school's endowments.

THREE HUNDRED YEARS ON

The man chosen to take the school into its fourth century was Edwin Merriman, the rector of All Saints and a master about whom not a bad word seems ever to have been spoken. When commissioners appointed by the House of Commons paid a visit in 1818 as part of a national enquiry into charities for the education of the poor, the Earl of Chichester (a trustee) assured them that he was 'very satisfied' with Merriman, whose 'merit alone procured him the presentation of the living of All Saints'.

The hard-nosed investigators were not to be deflected by warm words, however. We have a record of their interview with Merriman, in which they get to the heart of the school's finances and its teaching.

There were twelve free boys, he told them, and another fifteen private pupils boarding at his house, which could accommodate twenty-four. He lived in the house rent-free and was responsible for its upkeep. His income (itemised below) came from, respectively, the Jenkins, Morley and Blunt bequests and the invested proceeds from the sale of the Southover site.

'I receive annually the sum of £53 5s from Mr Shadwell of Hastings, who is Lord Chichester's steward. I also receive an annuity of £20 per annum from Mr Guy of Hammessey, who holds there a farm of Sir Charles Burrell. I receive £3 a year from Mr Verral a solicitor in Lewes, and also the interest of £479 0s 10d three per cent stock, which is paid to me at the Lewes bank, amounting to £14 7s 4d.'

'Do you appropriate all these payments to your own benefit?'

'I take the whole of them for my own use, but I pay an assistant, who is my curate, £150 a year; and I pay a writing master £25 a year; he lives in my house.

'There are twelve [students] who receive instruction gratuitously. They all come from the town of Lewes. They are taught the classics, and prepared for the universities. They are also instructed, without pay, in reading, writing and arithmetic by the writing master.'

'Are they found in books and stationery?'

'I make out a bill of what has been used by them, and if they or their friends choose to pay for them I receive it. Otherwise I do not exact it.'

SCHOOLS AT WAR

In 1779 William Gwynne was involved in a spat with Charles Cater Rand, who ran a rival boarding school with a strong scientific bent.

Gwynne had decided to drop the school's Whitsun break and replace it with a summer holiday from August to early September.

Cater Rand fired off a broadside, saying that he had consulted the parents and guardians 'of those young Gentlemen under his care', and that he would be sticking to the usual arrangements.

The grammar school won the day, however, and Cater Rand had to climb down in another public statement, altering the date of his school's own holiday and making what amounted to a grovelling apology:

'MR RAND would be very sorry for any Person to understand from his Advertisement that he means to insinuate any Thing slighting or, in the least Degree, prejudicial to Mr GWYNNE's Character.'

1820–30

*Reign of George IV
formerly Prince Regent*

1822

First gas lighting in Lewes

'Do you make any distinction between the free boys and your own private pupils?'

'None whatever. My senior boy is a free scholar and is going to the university next year. The free boys are the sons, generally, of the respectable inhabitants of Lewes. About six or seven years ago a man who kept a public house in Lewes applied to me to have his son admitted as a free boy; I told him what the course of instruction was and asked him for what his son was intended. After this I then heard no more about it.'

'Do you insist upon every free boy learning the classics as well as writing and accounts?'

'I do not. They may learn writing and accounts separately if they please. I think there has been one boy so instructed in my time.'

When the commissioners made their report the following year they expressed their unhappiness about the use of the charitable funds. They called for the number of trustees to be increased, no doubt in the hope that this might lead to better governance.

It occurs to us to observe, that as twelve was thought by those who manage Mrs Jenkins' foundation to be the proper number to be sent to the school under her benefaction only, there seems to be no scholar who can strictly be said to receive the benefits of Mrs Morley's bounty, which it is therefore impossible to say has been applied as that testatrix intended, unless it can be considered that the fund supplied by her has answered her general intention, in being made auxiliary to the free establishment under Mrs Jenkins' endowment.

It may be remarked further, that if all the free scholars at present in the school are to be looked upon as being there only upon Mrs Jenkins' foundation, the bills sent to their friends for books and stationery, though payment is said not to be insisted upon, can scarcely be considered as proper, there being £15 set apart by her for that purpose.

If, indeed, there were any boys who could be regarded as scholars on Mrs Morley's foundation, it must be admitted that her will affords some colour for making out such bills, under the words 'otherwise than of their benevolence'.

We understood upon inquiry that though the number of the scholars under Mrs Jenkins' foundation is limited to twelve by her trustees, that no limitation as to the number under Mrs Morley's foundation has been imposed by the trustees of her charity, and that this part of the school foundation is considered as open to the inhabitants of the town generally.

Whether this rap over the knuckles had any effect we don't know. Edwin Merriman was to serve the school, and his parish, for only two more years. The poor man died in 1821, having lingered for several months after falling down the stairs and breaking his back.

Now it was the turn of the Rev Dr George Proctor, who would eventually leave the school in the lurch.

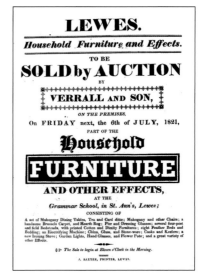

A poster advertising a sale at the grammar school in July, 1821, the year in which George Proctor became the headmaster. The furniture for sale included a set of mahogany dining tables, mahogany and other chairs, several 'four-post and field bedsteads', eight feather beds and an 'electrifying machine' – used for medical purposes.

Were the chairs and tables among the furniture left by Rev Graves (left), the remains of whose library Proctor had the constables remove?

The Graves' library scandal

In his will of 1717 the rector of St Peter and St Mary Westout, Rev Joseph Graves, bequeathed his remarkable library 'in trust for the benefit of the inhabitants of the town of Lewes'. He also left enough furniture for two rooms, no doubt hoping that his trustees would find suitable accommodation. Unhappily he provided no money to support his donation, and an enquiry by the Charity Commissioners more than a hundred years later uncovered a shameful story.

'The library, consisting of upwards of 500 volumes chiefly in divinity, many of them rare and valuable, appears from as far back as can be traced to have been deposited in the upper part of the grammar school house, where they seem to have been so entirely neglected and left open to plunder, that upon the appointment of the Rev G. Proctor, the late master, their number was reduced to little more than 100, and those of little value and for the most part in very bad condition, as was likely, the best having been purloined and the remainder taken no care of.'

The upshot was that Proctor had the constables remove the remaining books, and in 1823 they were sold to a London bookseller for just £53. They included a Walton's Polyglot Bible (in nine languages), but 'in the circumstances' this was the best price that could be obtained.

Edward Boys Ellman as a schoolboy

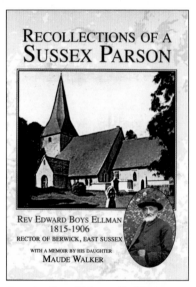

RECOLLECTIONS OF A
SUSSEX PARSON

REV EDWARD BOYS ELLMAN
1815-1906
RECTOR OF BERWICK, EAST SUSSEX

WITH A MEMOIR BY HIS DAUGHTER
MAUDE WALKER

Facsimile edition of Ellman's book published by Country Books in 2004

A PARSON REMEMBERS

The story of George Proctor's eight-year reign and its unhappy aftermath is colourfully told in the memoirs of Edward Boys Ellman (1815–1906), published after his death as *Recollections of a Sussex Parson*.

Ellman – who in later life was the vicar of Berwick, east of Lewes – joined the school as its youngest pupil just as it was recovering from a minor crisis. During Edwin Merriman's agonised last months his deputy Robert Airey had held the reins, but when he failed to get the job on a permanent basis he left to set up his own school in Brighton, taking many of the boys with him. Proctor was left with about thirty, a number which, chiefly by enrolling new boarders, he later increased to fifty.

Mentions of Ellman's schooling (for which, he tells us, he had little aptitude, especially the endless memorising of English, Greek and Latin texts) are scattered throughout the book. Excerpts are gathered together here to give an idea of what life was like for a Lewes grammar school pupil in the 1820s.

> In several cases the widows of officers and clergymen moved to Lewes on purpose for their sons to have the advantage of the Grammar School. I was one of the boys on the Foundation. The trustees of the school each had in turn to nominate a boy, and when Lord Hampden's turn arrived, in 1822, he offered my father the presentation for me, knowing that my two elder brothes were already at the school.
>
> I was tried with the Latin Grammar directly I went to school, but Mr Proctor soon saw it was advisable to wait a few months. I am convinced that it would have been wiser had I waited for years.
>
> Looking back after a long life, I see that a great part of my school life was misspent. Not that I was ever acccused of being idle, but I had the greatest difficulty in learning by heart, and ciphering I could not understand. My handwriting was never good, the canings and floggings that I daily received on my hands and arms I think accounted for that.
>
> I often misunderstood the directions given me. The consequence was that I was always at the bottom of my class, and rarely a day passed but what I received punishment. Proctor and the other masters were fond of the cane, and it was in constant use.

Being a day boy Proctor had no idea how much time I spent on my lessons. When ten years of age I was generally up till 10 or even 11 o'clock trying to learn them, and then frequently began again by 4am.

We had to be in school at 7am in the summer and 7.30 in the winter. We were allowed from 8.30 to 9.30 for breakfast, and from 12.30 till 2 for dinner, and then came out of school at half-past four. Much time was taken up in going backwards and forwards to Southover. I rarely joined in a game of play, and when I have had an offer of going to an evening's entertainment I have positively refused, saying I must learn my lessons. Competition certainly never answered in my case, and it was only when I was released from working in class and allowed to go my own pace that I got on.

I leave on record this account of my own school days as a warning against making mistakes in the instruction of children, from the teacher not understanding the child, or the child not undestanding the teacher. Idleness, obstinacy or some other fault is ascribed to a child, and the child feels it keenly in after years.

One day I had to learn from the Eton grammar a long rule of syntax. I stopped up till 11 the night before trying to master it, when my mother would not let me stay up any longer, but I was down by 4 o'clock the next morning and went on poring over it till it was time to start for school.

Whilst I was getting ready my brother Frederic took up my school-bag in mistake for his own and started without me. As soon as I was ready I missed my bag and went hunting about after it, and said I could not go to school without it. I was still searching when Frederic came home for breakfast and explained his mistake.

When I went to school after breakfast Proctor evidently thought I had stopped away to escape the lesson, so he tried me, and finding I did not know it, told me to stop in school till the afternoon and threatened to flog me severely if I did not say it correctly then.

I was so frightened by the threat and his manner that I did not even notice that I was not to go home, and felt confident that I must submit to the flogging, for I felt sure I could never say it perfectly. So I did not stop in, and on going back to school in the afternoon got a most severe flogging, Mr Proctor supposing I had wilfully disobeyed him.

THE SADDLER'S SON

A poignant story from Ellman's book:

'The class of boys, with I think only two exceptions, consisted of the sons of the clergy, retired officers, solicitors, bankers, doctors etc.

One of the exceptions was a remarkably clever lad named Saxby, son of a saddler living in Lewes, who promised well, and whose father Proctor urged to allow the boy to go to the University. But the father objected to raise his son above the position to which he was born, and would not consent.

It is hardly to be expected that he would have risen as high as the present Bishop of Gloucester, who was a saddler's son from Gloucester. But it seemed a great pity that one who as a boy far excelled his companions in Greek and Latin should afterwards be seen stitching saddles in his father's shop, as I often saw him doing when on my way home from school.'

1830–37
Reign of William IV

1830
'Swing riots' in protest against agricultural depression

1832
First Reform Bill; John Every establishes the Phoenix Ironworks in Lewes

1833
Slavery abolished throughout British Empire

1836 – December 24
Eight people killed in Britain's worst avalanche disaster, at Lewes

Contemporary painting of the avalanche, now in Anne of Cleves House museum

SPIRITED AWAY

And then, in 1829, Dr Proctor (by now rector of St Michael's) suddenly played Pied Piper and stole the children away. What he did was accept the headship of Elizabeth College in Guernsey, then being rebuilt, and urge parents to let their sons board the steamboat with him. Several of them obliged, Ellman's included.

Proctor didn't stay long in the Channel Islands. He fell out with the governors, and within three years he was back in Sussex. This was to be of no benefit to the grammar school, however, because he took over a rival academy in Brighton – Chichester House in Kemp Town – and Ellman, now sixteen, was one of the boys who followed him there rather than return to Lewes.

'Proctor was always successful in getting pupils,' he wrote, 'and very soon had as many as he could take, amongst others Henry Gage and George Shiffner, both of whom were put by their fathers under my protection, in the same way that Henry Gage's father, Lord Gage, had been under my father's.'

The Dickens of a headmaster

Charles Dickens wrote parts of *Dombey and Son* while staying at the Bedford Hotel in Brighton and is said to have taken George Proctor as the model for Dr Blimber, at whose rigorous academy the young Paul Dombey labours at Latin and Greek until his death at the age of six.

Dr Blimber and his young charges as drawn for Dickens by Phiz.

'The doctor was a portly gentleman in a suit of black,' we read. 'He had a bald head, highly polished; a deep voice; and a chin so very double that it was a wonder how he ever managed to shave into the creases.'

His teaching regime would certainly have been recognised by Edward Boys Ellman. The school is described as 'a great hot-house in which there was a forcing apparatus incessantly at work. All the boys blew before their time.'

Dr Proctor was followed as headmaster of the grammar school by Charles Williams (another man of the cloth, of course), who cut costs to make ends meet. According to Ellman 'he kept such a poor table, nearly starving the boys, that he had but few boarders. My younger brother, Harvey, was one who had to be removed very ill with a sort of fever, brought on by want of sufficient food.'

The school was in crisis. Ellman, looking back years later, blamed electoral bribery reminiscent of the Whigs *v* Tories era: 'The cause of the dwindling of the school was (in my estimation) principally the First Reform Bill, which made Parliamentary voters of every £10 householder, and consequently boys were appointed to the Foundation to secure their fathers' votes; and a class of boys were admitted which lowered the whole stamp of the old Grammar School. Consequently the upper classes of the Lewes residents sent their boys elsewhere.'

AN INSPECTOR CALLS

Williams was still in charge when the Charity Commissioners came knocking once again. Their verdict was utterly damning. In headline form, this is what they found:

- *The headmaster operated 'without control and without responsibility'*

- *The trustees were absentees whose only interest was in taking turn to appoint the boys – sometimes their own*

- *On admittance, 'no interest was taken in the children's ability or condition, or of their parents'*

- *The school gave much more attention to fee-paying pupils than to the free boys*

- *No minute book had been kept by the trustees, 'or any account of their disbursements'*

- *No Southover boys had been admitted for thirty years*

Unsurprisingly, the commissioners called for the school's complete reorganisation and more openness, adding that there should be equal numbers of Lewes and Southover boys.

A SHOCK AT OXFORD

Edward Boys Ellman went up to Wadham College, Oxford, despite his chequered school career, but he had a bit of a shock when he applied.

'I was asked what I had read, and I mentioned among others Aeschylus and Sophocles.

'The conclusion arrived at, after the examination, was that I was very badly grounded, and that Proctor's system (under which I had been for twelve years) must have been decidedly wrong.'

1837–1901
Reign of Queen Victoria

1837
Sussex Agricultural Express
(*later the* Sussex Express)
founded

1845
*Brighton College opens – first
public school in Sussex*

NOT FIT FOR PURPOSE

Once a new building was
proposed everyone felt
free to attack the old one.
'We despise its mean
accommodations,' sniffed
the *Sussex Agricultural
Express*, 'its curious
rooms, ingeniously
contrived and shaped, as
it were, to be inconvenient
to everyone; its queer
corners, its absence of
ventilation and its narrow
school room with its
deeply rather than
elaborately carved desks.'

The report was published in 1839, and their comments were
so waspish that some of the criticisms demand to be produced in
full. They began with a brief history of the school, coming to the
time when it moved up to St Anne's. Their interpretation of
Agnes Morley's will was that she intended her gift to be enjoyed
solely by the children of Southover.

> The distance and the difficulty of reaching the school at Lewes
> in winter induced many [Southover] parents to discontinue
> sending their children, and an undue preference having in
> other instances been given to the children of Lewes, till in
> process of the time the number of 12 was filled by Lewes
> boys, and the free grammar-school was effectually annihilated,
> and all the benefit of education arising from it imperceptibly
> transferred to the children of Lewes, to the entire exclusion
> of those of Southover, for whom alone it was intended, not a
> single boy from Southover having been admitted to it for the
> last 30 years.
>
> It was urged that the parishioners of Southover made no
> application for admittance on the part of their children. The
> reason for this might be that there was no chance of its being
> successful. Lewes being a borough town, for which they had
> no vote, they were not likely to prevail against competition
> that *had*. As they have never ceased to complain of being
> deprived of all benefit from the free grammar school, they
> would no doubt have urged their claim could they have done
> so with effect.

The present master, the report continued, 'does not insist
upon the free boys learning the classics, but permits them, if
it is the wish of the parents, to learn the other branches
exclusively.' He had five boarders paying £52 10s a year, five day
scholars paying £10 10s a year and there were twelve free boys.

> This is a most objectionable system. Ten guineas a year for
> the day scholars is much too high, and the number of free
> scholars ought to be enlarged. The trustees have no power to
> limit it to twelve. It has no doubt been restricted by the master,
> whose interest it is that the least possible number should be
> admitted to the foundation because, that number being filled
> up, he makes a charge of ten guineas a year for all beyond it.

We are justified in assuming that it is in this free school, as it is in many others where the practice of receiving pay-scholars prevails, that the chief attention is employed in the instruction of those who pay while little concern is shown about such as do not pay. That portion of the income which was to be applied in the purchase of books for the children is not so applied, and their parents are obliged to pay for them.

The trustees of this Free Grammar School have usually been resident at a very considerable distance from Lewes, and have manifested no interest in it beyond the appointment of the boys, which has been made a source of private patronage, each trustee taking the nomination in turn.

Upon every vacancy the child whose friends possess the greatest interest is appointed; numerous intances having been mentioned of children being admitted whose parents were well able to pay for their education, and in some intances the trustees have appointed their own children, all of which is a manifest perversion of the endowment.

What was to be done? By the time Mark Antony Lower published the first edition of *A Hand-book for Lewes* around 1845 Charles Williams had been replaced as master by the Rev James Cary, 'son of the learned translator of Dante'. Dr Cary seems to have got his teaching right, because a local paper reported some time later that one of his students had been awarded a first in mathematics at Oxford, with another three getting BAs at the university in the same year.

Whether the specific issues raised by the commissioners had been addressed we don't know, but the *Hand-book* was scathing about the school building, which it described as 'an old house of uninviting aspect'.

Optimistic well-wishers now seized upon an attractive remedy for the institution's well documented failings: they would knock the place down and start again!

The word spread around the town, volunteers came forward and the Committee for Promoting the Restoration of the Lewes Free Grammar School duly held its first meeting on December 6th, 1848.

CHIMNEY POT CRICKET

In his memoirs, written around 1910, George Chambers, recalls the cricketing enthusiasm of Dr Cary.

Chambers was a pupil at Chichester House School in Brighton, where Carey had gone after his headship at Lewes.

'Dr Cary,' he writes, 'was not only an active player, considering his age (which was much over 50), but he was keen at watching the game when great matches were in progress.

'He himself always played in a "chimney pot" hat, which was the full-dress headgear in those days, though it was permissible for boys to wear flannel skull caps with peaks.

'Once or twice we were taken for special "treats" over to Lewes to meet a Lewes team at the Dripping Pan.'

1846

Railway comes to Lewes; founding of the Sussex Archaeological Society; repeal of the Corn Laws

The original railway station in Friars Walk, on the site which later housed the local magistrates' court

A BUILDER'S WHIM

The present school was built in 1851 on the site it had occupied since around 1714. The builder, like his medieval counterparts, couldn't resist adding a curious embellishment to the west wall. The little face is weather-worn today, but still visible if you look closely.

The building originally had three gables, rather than today's two.

A New Beginning?

EVERY GOOD CAUSE needs a champion, and the grammar school now found one in William Edwin Baxter. With the school's own coffers bare, the only way to pay for a new building was through public subscription – and this wasn't a good time to put out the begging bowl. The agricultural depression of the 1830s and 40s had taken its toll on Lewes, once the brisk trading centre for weald and downland farmers, and the arrival of the railway in Sussex was luring trade, industry and 'the fashion' to rival towns such as Brighton and Eastbourne.

The grammar school trustees were headed by the Earl of Chichester, with Sir Henry Shiffner at his right hand, but the gritty business of fund-raising was delegated to a sub-committee of half a dozen less elevated mortals. Among them, cannily, were two newspaper editors: Baxter of the *Sussex Agricultural Express* and G.F. Bacon of the *Sussex Advertiser* – a rival which, since a fire six years earlier, Baxter had generously allowed to use his own presses.

Their first public statement called for contributions totalling £2,000, offering the carrot of adding a further eight places to the foundation, either free or for 'a trifling annual fee'. It argued the school's case, and explained its predicament:

> It has long been a subject of regret to those interested in the welfare of the town, that a place consisting of at least 10,000 inhabitants should be destitute of a good public school. Other towns of far less importance are amply provided with the means of offering a liberal education to all who will accept it, either gratuitously or on payment of a small annual sum, through the munificence of founders and benefactors.
>
> But Lewes, although possessing an endowed grammar school, is really unprovided with effective machinery for supplying, according to the benevolent intention of its founder, a sound classical and mathematical education.
>
> The amount of the original endowment made in the year 1512 remains stationary, being in the form of a fixed real charge, and is subsquently incapable of furnishing funds for enlarging the charity or repairing the school premises.

MEET THE BAXTERS

In 1802 the printer and publisher John Baxter set up his press at the top of School Hill. The inventor of an advanced inking roller, he published a variety of books, among them the 'Baxter Bible' and Horsfield's histories of Lewes and Sussex.

One son, George, is regarded as the inventor of colour printing. He went his own way, creating the famous 'Baxter prints' which were all the rage at the Great Exhibition in London in 1851.

Another son, William, joined his father's print business, which became W.E. Baxter. Together they launched the *Sussex Agricultural Express* (later the *Sussex Express*), with William as its editor.

William's son Wynne (*page 53*) was to become the first mayor of Lewes, before making a name beyond the town.

THE FIRST ENEMY OF BONFIRE

G.F. Bacon, who as editor of the *Sussex Advertiser* played an active part in promoting the restoration of the school, has the dubious distinction of being the town's very first 'enemy of Bonfire'.

In 1850 the Pope restored the hierarchy of Roman Catholic bishops in England, and this provoked violent scenes on November 5th. While the *Express* took a Tory stance, suspicious of the Catholic revival, the *Advertiser* had been a voice of toleration at a time when the Liberal element in the town was attempting to suppress the excesses of Bonfire.

Bacon's name proved irresistible to the Bonfire Boys. As his newspaper reported, an effigy of the Pope was consigned to the flames along with 'an ingenious representation of the editor of this journal in the shape of a pig'.

A subsequent benefaction in the year 1709 yields so small a return even when added to the above endowment as scarcely to afford gratuitous instruction to 12 scholars. And the school buildings are in such a ruinous condition, from the lapse of time and natural decay, that unless immediate steps be taken to the effectual restoration the main object of the institution will be in a great measure frustrated.

William Baxter had a personal reason for wanting the school to succeed: his son Wynne was a pupil, and the rather overblown praise of the institution in some of his subsequent reports suggests very strongly that he had been educated there himself.

Throughout 1849 the *Express* kept potential contributors on their toes. As early as that January it was obvious that the campaigners had a struggle on their hands. Baxter and his five colleagues reported to their committee that 'in consequence of the depressed state of the times, the subscriptions have not amounted to so large a sum as was originally anticipated'. The minutes reveal that they therefore felt 'compelled to forego their first intention of erecting so expensive a building'.

Their public stance was rather more bullish. The paper published regular lists of individual donations, with the Earl of Abergavenny having 'most liberally subscribed £100' and 'Master Wythes (a pupil)' giving £5. The edition of March 3rd reported that half the required sum had already been raised and that it was hoped to begin building by mid-summer.

The school now had a new headmaster. The Rev Charles Stroud Green was installed as the rector of St Anne's in December, 1948, and he was one of the early donors, putting up £50. Lewes Old Bank had given the same, while the Earl of Chichester and Lt Gen the Hon H. Trevor at Glynde were both in for £20. The appearance of 'J. Davey, builder £5' on an early list proved to be significant, because Joseph Davey's plans for the new school would be chosen ahead of 'several of very great merit' – and some, unfortunately, which would have proved far too expensive.

Baxter wasn't shy of using moral blackmail. Here he is in April 1849, twisting the arms of the two local MPs.

> Our worthy representatives – the Hon H. Fitzroy and R. Perfect Esq – in their recent visit to their constituents, expressed, we understand, their warm approbation of the undertaking, and we have every reason to believe they will become, upon application, very liberal supporters.
>
> We mention this lest our townsfolk should feel any surprise at the omission of their names from the list of patrons.

Mid-summer came and went. Some who had promised to subscribe had yet to cough up, and in October the trustees decided, privately, that they would 'not be justified in suffering the present school to be disturbed until the sum of one thousand and eight hundred pounds is subscribed and paid into the hands of the treasurer'. (Davey's final bill would be for £1,703 13s 6d.)

Charles Green saved the day. He put a further £200 into the pot and the immediate target was reached. The headmaster would make five separate contributions in all, amounting to £550 – almost a third of the total sum raised, and in those days a very substantial sum. The old building was demolished.

PRIMING THE PUMP

Still a relentless pressure was applied on the goodwill of the local populace. Readers were told, among much else, that the revived school would encourage families to settle in the neighbourhood, and therefore be good for businesses, the professions and trade.

20/10/49 The appeal is 'within £100 or £150' of the target, and contributions, 'however small' can be deposited at the *Express* office or the Old Bank

9/2/50 'Certain influential inhabitants of this Town have, in accordance with the suggestion set forth in the lecture at the County Hall last week, formed themselves into a committee who will undertake to call upon the respectable inhabitants of Lewes in behalf of the grammar school fund. Enough money has been raised to allow of three feet additional pitch being given to the school room, and to permit of it being lengthened to 50 feet.'

LAYING THE FOUNDATION STONE OF THE BOROUGH OF LEWES FREE GRAMMAR SCHOOL.

Report in the Express *of the laying of the foundation stone on March 21st, 1850. 'We are not certain that we have ever recorded the destruction of the Old Grammar School,' it reads. 'Scarcely one stone, however, of the edifice has been left standing on another for many months.'*

SUB-COMMITTEE REPORT

'Care has been taken to secure a spacious and well ventilated schoolroom capable of containing at least one hundred boys; and in the event of an increase in boarders, five additional chambers can be fitted up for their reception at a trifling cost.'

'The workmen engaged in the erection were not forgotten, but had a good substantial dinner provided for them at the Black Horse Inn, Western Road, accompanied with a liberal supply of beer.

The men were much gratified with their treat, especially the excellent manner in which the dinner was sent up by the worthy landlady, Mrs Smith.'

* 'Alas, Posthumus, the fleeting years slip by.' The line from the Latin poet Horace was a standard part of grammar school study

2/3/50 'Among other excellent ideas in connection with the establishment, we hear of a proposal to raise a neat and roomy *shed*, which shall extend a considerable length along the side of the playground so that in foul weather the boys may not be deprived of exercise to very requisite for the enjoyment of sound health, whether of mind or body.' (More money was still needed and existing donors were asked to consider making second or third contributions.)

LAYING THE STONE

The publicity drive continued during the great stone-laying ceremony on March 21st. This was covered by the *Express* with all the pomp – and, indeed, pomposity – expected of a grand Victorian occasion.

Let us bid adieu then to the old schoolhouse, whilst chronicling what we deem its defects, in all friendliness of feeling! Many of us have known it as the scene of joys and sorrows which were once to us everything, and the new building, standing as it does on the old site of our boyish tasks and sports, will still be to us the Lewes Grammar School, and remind us, as age creeps on, of that beautiful lament over the lapse of time, so often to be heard, now, as then, within its walls:

'Eheu! fagaces, Posthume! Posthume!
Labuntur anni.'*

The old building, as we have said, is gone, but the wreck of the past and the preparations for the future crowd the site in what appears to the uninitiated a dreadfully confused state. Bricks, and earth, and mortar, were in heaps on every side, and for the narrow dimensions of a pathway cleared for the occasion the fashionable dresses of the ladies, who began to arrive between twelve and one, were 'a world too wide'. In one corner of the ground a shed had been erected, and slightly covered, and in this the parties took refuge from the cutting wind of a cold March morning.

Immediately opposite, a large excavation had been made, about which the foundations stone of the new building was suspended. Round this, taking their stand on a sort of spoil-bank, stood a number of spectators, and from this spot the addresses were afterwards given.

The 'noble lord' (Chichester) made a speech – which inevitably included an appeal for more funds – before taking a trowel from Joseph Davey, lowering a bottle of Victorian coins and a parchment inscribed with a dedication in Latin into an allotted hole and mortaring the foundation stone in place in 'a workmanlike manner'.

After more orotund speeches 'the party broke up and repaired to the Star Hotel where an excellent luncheon had been prepared by Mr Jones'. More speeches followed, with a vote of thanks to the two journalists, Baxter and Bacon.

The earl of Chichester expressed his esteem for the Rev Green, and was unable to resist a little homily. As the *Express* reported:

> The education which was now bestowed upon the lower classes, and which he thought was a matter for congratulation, had had a very satisfactory influence on the classes above them.
>
> One peculiarity of the present day was that there was not only a greater desire for the extension of education and the cultivation of the higher branches of learning but, which was far more important, there was a general anxiety that it should be conducted by men of sound religious principles.

Master Fuller wins the day

The star of the occasion was the senior boy on the foundation, 'Master Henry Fuller', who made an impressive speech littered with the required Latin phrases, before demanding that the event's anniversary be henceforward celebrated as a free day for ever.

'You must fling down your weapons of defence, my lord,' he addressed the Earl of Chichester, and confess "Veni, vidi sed non vici".* Proclaim, "Boys, the 21st of March shall be an annual holiday in the calendar of the Lewes Grammar School" and further, "Esto perpetua!"‡ '

The good earl, presumably forewarned, agreed to this request, and it was decided that if the free day fell on a Sunday the boys should have the Monday off instead.

A HEAD'S AMBITION

In his luncheon speech Charles Green spoke of the benefits of a classical and mathematical education, but also stressed the importance of religion.

'I shall be perfectly content if the school over which I have been called to preside maintain a respectable position among provincial grammar schools by sending forth an average number of sound scholars and good Christians.'

He also promised that he would show no favouritism.

'Whatever honours or rewards it is in our power to bestow shall be given to the best scholar and the best conducted boy without fear or favour.'

---

* *'I came, I saw but I did not conquer.'*
‡ *'May it last for ever!'*

1851
Opening of the new grammar school building

1853
Lewes prison opens

1859
Publication of Darwin's Origin of Species

1867
Second Reform Bill extends franchise to male urban working classes; publication of Marx's Das Kapital

1868
First premierships of Disraeli and Gladstone

1869
Endowed Schools Act

William Baxter's family grave in All Saints churchyard. He died in 1873.

BUSINESS AS USUAL

The *Express* had referred to the raising of a new building on the site as 'this new endowment of the Lewes Grammar School, for so only can it be termed'. It was, however, an endowment of brick and flint, with no extra income – and, as we have seen, the campaigners for the 'restored' school emphasised at the outset that the income from its earlier bequests was inadequate.

Charles Green remained headmaster until 1859 when, as graphically described by Edward Boys Ellman, he was 'starved to death by ossification of the throat, which, gradually closing, prevented his taking food.' How much he felt the financial pinch during those years we don't know, but a crisis duly arrived during the stewardship of Frederic Woolley, the rector of St Michael's.

Ellman, who regretted not contributing to the building fund ('As I was at the time rebuilding Berwick rectory I had not a guinea to spare'), later wrote that under Woolley the numbers at

A study in flint

An outstanding feature of the 1851 'neo-Tudor' school is its frontage of knapped flints. They match those of the three buildings next door, which include Tyne House and St Clair House, now also part of the school.

Courses of knapped flints above an arch.

Flints from the chalk are widely used in Lewes, often crudely, albeit attractively, in garden walls. Knapping (or finely chipping to shape) is a skill which allows the builder to run the flints in courses, as with bricks.

The architectural historian Alec Clifton-Taylor has written that nos 139–141 'provide an object lesson in flint construction'. He notes that the rough top storey of Tyne House was obviously a later addition, adding: 'The rest is excellent, with carefully coursed flints, many of them almost egg-shaped, and beautifully pointed brick surrounds to all the windows, not to mention the delightful doorway with its eliptically-arched fanlight.'

the school 'gradually dwindled, till his only pupil was his own son.' This is almost certainly a misremembering. The trustees' (sporadically kept) minutes show that in 1860, soon after he took over, there were just seven boys on the foundation, three paying boys from the town and sixteen boarders, some of whom were from Lewes. Shortly after his early death in 1877 there were 'three scholars in addition to the foundationers', and since a vacancy was reported on the foundation, it's reasonable to assume that there had recently been a full complement.

BROUGHT TO BOOK

A crisis there undoubtedly was, however, and the first outwards signs of it followed a visit by the Schools Inquiry Commission (*see panel, right*). By this time Woolley's health was failing. He had raised the number of pupils to 51 soon after arriving, but this was already down to 23 – in a building designed to cater for a hundred.

In short, the investigators found the school in very bad heart, and, like the charity commissioners twenty-five years before, they were scathing about the trustees:

- *These 'noblemen and country gentlemen' limited their functions to appointing the master and nominally the 12 foundation scholars'*

- *They had held no meeting for seven years*

- *Two of them had shown 'occasional interest' in the school*

As for Charles Green's policy of non-favouritism, a day boy, if he was 'a nice lad', was allowed to play with the boarders in the playground which, having been the garden for the exclusive use of the master, was entirely under his control.

Woolley soldiered on – in one sense literally. He joined the ranks of the 4th Sussex Rifle Volunteers, and he drilled with them until he was appointed chaplain to the corps. It's perhaps an indication of his priorities that his obituary in the *Express* spoke of his parish work and his sermons to the volunteers ('marked with originality and earnestness') but made no mention of his being headmaster of Lewes Grammar School.

Weatherworn sign on the school wall showing the dates 1512 and 1851.

THE TAUNTON REPORT

The Victorians made education a priority, and poorly run schools found it increasingly difficult to hide their failings.

Between 1864 and 1868 the Schools Inquiry Commission under Lord Taunton investigated 782 grammar schools, plus some proprietary and private schools, and found that the provision of secondary education was poor and unevenly distributed, two-thirds of English towns having no secondary schools of any kind.

The Endowed Schools Act created a commission with considerable powers to improve standards of education for both boys and girls. In 1874 it was merged into the Charity Commission.

He died at the age of 55, leaving a widow and four children, and the school did, briefly, feature in the paper's account of his funeral. 'The body enclosed in a coffin covered with a black cloth, and having furniture of the same sombre hue, was borne from the Grammar School shortly before half past twelve.' Most shops in the town closed out of respect, and 'the blinds of private houses were drawn down'.

ANOTHER BAXTER ENTERS THE FRAY

Now the trustees at last stirred themselves, introducing new blood to their number in what was to become a desperate attempt to revive the school's wilting fortunes. Even then, though, they managed to handle things clumsily. In the same issue of the newspaper as the funeral report a strongly worded letter from Wynne Baxter condemned the fact that the identities of the new trustees remained a secret.

Baxter, son of the former *Express* editor and at this time the Sussex coroner, rode to the attempted rescue of his old school just as his father had done before him. He urged the town's high constables to call a pubic meeting to debate the school's affairs, and expressed the hope that 'a new scheme will be asked of the Charity Commissioners, and that, with the cooperation of all parties, the grammar school may be once more a credit to the old borough'.

He noted that the school was short of money and made an interesting suggestion – that its endowments should be combined with those of Steere's charity (*page 25*) in order to provide it with more financial security. It was to be a suggestion with fateful consequences.

Memorial to Frederic Woolley in St Michael's church

WYNNE EDWIN BAXTER *Coroner*

A solicitor, translator, antiquarian and plant collector, Wynne E. Baxter (1844–1920) was also the first mayor of Lewes, but he's best known for his role as a coroner in many high profile legal cases – the most sensational of them all being the 'Jack the Ripper' killings in 1888.

Baxter in his mayoral robes.

He first set up a practice in Lewes, and in 1881, as Sussex coroner, he investigated the death of the Balcombe Tunnel murder victim Frederick Gold and presided over the inquest of the man who hanged for the crime, Percy Lefroy Mapleton.

While maintaining his practice in Lewes, he moved to London, where he opened a solicitor's office and advertising agency. By 1885 he held the deputy coronerships of the City of London and the borough of Southwark, and a year later he was elected to his first full coroner's post. Known as 'the father of London coroners', he used the telegram address 'Inquest London'.

In the absence of a court case (nobody was ever charged) he played a vital role in investigating the gruesome Whitechapel murders. He was renowned for his sharp interviewing technique, but revealed his compassionate side when addressing the jury about one of the Ripper's victims:

'She lived principally in the common lodging houses in the neighbourhood of Spitalfields, where such as she herd like cattle, and she showed signs of great deprivation, as if she had been badly fed.

'The glimpses of life in these dens which the evidence in this case discloses is sufficient to make us feel that there is much in the nineteenth century civilisation of which we have small reason to be proud; but you who are constantly called together to hear the sad tale of starvation, or semi-starvation, of misery, immorality, and wickedness which some of the occupants of the 5,000 beds in this district have every week to relate to coroners' inquests, do not require to be reminded of what life in a Spitalfields lodging-house means.'

His many other cases included the inquest into the death of the so-called Elephant Man, Joseph Merrick, in 1890, while during the first world war he investigated the deaths of German spies and the victims of German air raids.

'I have held over 30,000 inquests,' he once commented proudly, 'and have not had one body exhumed yet.'

Wynne Baxter's name lives on in the solicitors' practice based in Bell Lane.

AMATEUR DRAMATIC PERFORMANCE.

GRAMMAR SCHOOL

LEWES.

POSITIVELY FOR TWO NIGHTS ONLY.

Wednesday & Thursday, Dec. 27 & 28, 1871.

On WEDNESDAY, Dec. 27th, the Performance will commence with the
Burlesque of

BOMBASTES FURIOSO.

Artaxominous (King of Utopia) ... ... Mr. G. Bushby.
Fusbos (Minister of State) ... ... Mr. R. Rosseter.
General Bombastes ... ... Mr. H. Molineux.
Distaffina ... ... Miss Leslie.

Soldiers, Courtiers, &c.

Scene 1. INTERIOR OF THE PALACE.
Scene 2. A WOOD.
Scene 3. DISTAFFINA'S COTTAGE.
Scene 4. A WOOD.

*Playbill for a theatrical
production at the school,
Christmas 1871 [ESRO]*

But what was a modern grammar school education *for*? That was the question posed in the next edition of the *Express* in reply to Baxter's letter. The writer was Charles Parsons, who styled himself as 'Lewes born and bred', who lived in East Street and who had been educated at the school for six years.

A modern school, he said, should teach mathematics, science, modern languages, literature and history. Those who wanted a classical education sent their children to one of the great public schools. Lewes Grammar School needed to make up its mind whether to become another Eton 'or cease to make the classics the staple of what it teaches'. Frederic Woolley, he added, *had* wanted a 'modern side' for the school.

> The school should, if possible, fulfil its proper function more satisfactorily than it has done for some time past.
>
> As to the cause, I believe it is to be found mainly not in personal or purely local conditions, but in the great change which has come over the educational system in the country. The old grammar schools are, in most places, played out. A grammar school is no longer wanted in Lewes for several reasons.
>
> It must, therefore, be converted into a middle class school [in which] practical men of business would be no longer exasperated at finding their sons deeply learned in the wisdom of the ancients, but quite incapable of making out a bill or doing a sum in compound interest.

A complete overhaul of the school's philosophy was no doubt beyond trustees trying to cope with the basic task of keeping the institution going, but the letter must have touched a nerve. Had their kind of teaching become an irrelevance? Should they change direction?

What they did immediately was ask for a report on the condition of the school building (it was 'in a fair state of repair', as after only twenty-six years it surely ought to have been); write a letter to the Charity Commissioners, suggesting 'a scheme' for amalgamating all the local educational charities; and advertise for a new headmaster.

The man they chose was a 37-year-old Canadian, the Rev Charles Badgley. A doctor's son, he had studied at Queen's College,

Oxford, and worked as an assisant master at the forerunner of Hurstpierpoint College before returning home to apply the English public school ethos to the new, nine-pupil Trinity College School in Ontario. The recollections of boys who studied under him there give us a portrait of the man chosen to steady the grammar school ship as it pitched and tossed in choppy waters.

The headmaster was good nature itself, notwithstanding that he sometimes wore a fierce look. He was very dark, and his clean-shaven face showed distinctly the area which he was obliged to traverse every morning. He had piercing black eyes and straight and somewhat lowering eyebrows, which gave a stern appearance to the upper part of his face. But around the mouth there was a lurking expression of humour which at times completely offset the sternness of his face.

Boys generally can discover the weak spot in a man's character, and they are just as astute in discovering how to take advantage of it. Many a half-holiday was secured by watching the lower part of the Head's face, and striking for liberty when it was apparent that the feeling indexed by the lower part were stronger than those indexed by the upper part. The concession, however, was always accompanied by a sternly pronounced condition that the half-holiday should be devoted to football or cricket, according to season.

Although the Head could wield a cane with skill and effect, he relied more upon the honour of the boys than their fear of punishment, and on his moral influence rather than his compulsory powers. His influence was very great.

He was an excellent classical scholar and teacher. The tone of the school was largely due to his ideas of discipline and schoolboy honour, which at that time were extremely new to me. Like many other schoolboys I used to regard all masters as the natural enemies of boys, their official torturers. The idea of a master being companionable to a boy, being of assistance to him, being anxious for, or even desirous of, his welfare, or believing that there was anything good in a boy, had never entered into my notion of the realm of possibility. The effect of this policy on the boys was marvellous. Bad language and untruthfulness were almost unknown.

A HEAD TICKED OFF

Soon after Rev Charles. Badgley was appointed headmaster in 1877 he reported a vacancy in the foundation because of 'the continued absence of the boy Arthur Whilsed Bland'.

Whatever his reasons, the young absentee was duly struck from the roll – but Badgley was himself later rebuked for absence by the school's managers, as their minutes reveal:

23/1/1880
The committee of management desire to represent to the head-master their opinion that it is essential to the well-being of the school that he should be personally present during the school hours.

15/11/80
It is the opinion of the committee that during school hours the boys should be always under the superintendence of the headmaster, and that the hon secretary be requested to forward to the headmaster a copy of the resolution.

1881

Lewes, Southover and Cliffe incoporated into a borough, with Wynne Baxter as its first mayor

Borough coat of arms

MR BLAKER REGRETS

From Nathaniel Paine Blaker's *Sussex in Bygone Days*, published in 1906:

'Of all the changes which have taken place in Lewes during the last few years, not one perhaps has caused deeper regret than the disendowment of the old Grammar School.

When I first knew Lewes its reputation stood high, and many of the older men of the present generation received at all events much of their education at that school.'

Despite the evidence of these glowing Canadian testimonials, Charles Badgley was unable to work his magic on the grammar school. In January 1880 there were twelve boys on the foundation (repeated criticisms had presumably borne fruit), but only a further eleven day boys and one boarder. Judging by his own absences from the premises (*page 55*), he had lost his belief in the enterprise, and the following April he resigned.

LAST RITES

Events now moved swiftly. Wynne Baxter (the town's last high constable, and about to elected its first mayor) attended a trustees meeting that same month and made a general statement about the Blunt and Steere charities 'and the possibility of appropriating parts thereof to the endowment of the grammar school'.

Ominously, the trustees decided not to appoint a successor to Badgley 'pending a response from the Charity Commissioners'.

In June 1881 Francis Fearon, the Commissioners' nationally respected representative, visited the trustees to spell out the options available to them. The minutes of the meeting include the shocking relevation that only thirty years since its opening the school building was regarded as not fit for purpose – partly, it seems, because the boys were being taught in one large hall, rather than in individual classrooms.

> He stated that three courses seemed open to the trustees – viz – that if the trustees were desirous of making it a high class school in accordance with the scheme before them, the Commissioners would require the buildings to be put into thorough repair and classrooms to be built so as to make it meet modern requirements. Or, failing to do this, make it a second- or third-rate school or, finally, to close the school and devote the increase to exhibitions.
>
> Whereupon it was proposed by Mr Crosskey, seconded by Mr Turner and resolved:
>
> That a request be made to the Charity Commissioners that the Lewes Grammar School be closed after the pending summer term for a short time in order than at endeavour be made to raise funds to make such alterations and additions to the school premises as are necessary before the scheme submitted by the trustees can be approved by the Commissioners.

Four months later the Charity Commissioners consented to the closing of the school for a period of six months. Yet although an appeal for fresh funds fell on deaf ears (potential donors must have felt that they had heard it all before), the trustees still lived in hope: a deputation went up to London to argue the case for the school's future.

The Commissioners delivered their verdict in a letter dated December 5th, 1882. It must have been opened with trembling hands.

> The Commissioners do not, after careful consideration of what was alleged on that occasion by the deputation, think it to be desirable that the school should at present be re-opened, and that, in view of the failure of the recent effort to raise by subscription a fund for the improvement of the school buildings and augmentation of its endowment, and in default of any other source from which those objects can be accomplished, they now propose to prepare a scheme under the provision of the Endowed Schools Acts for the conversion of the Foundation into an Exhibition Fund.

It was a horrible blow. Wynne Baxter's idea of amalgamating all the Lewes educational charities had, indeed, won approval, but the trustees should have been wary of what they wished for. All the school's assets (not only its ancient endowments, but the very building itself) were to be stripped away and handed over to the new exhibition fund.

The good news for the neutral observer was that the fund would be available to the children of the town as a whole (girls as well as boys), and would benefit the brightest pupils and the best schools.

The bad news for Lewes Grammar School was that it would continue to exist, in name and in spirit, only if some brave soul shouldered the risk of renting the already ramshackle building in St Anne's. He would need ability, determination and no doubt a large slice of luck – and he would be on his own.

Charles Badgley. His pupils watched the lower part of his stern face before deciding to 'strike for liberty'.

Francis Fearon, the assistant commissioner who spelt out the options open to the school's trustees.

1884

*Third reform bill; franchise
for male rural working classes*

1885

Lewes Football Club founded

1888

County councils formed

1890

*Free elementary education
in England*

1893

Present town hall opens

*Right: Two entries from
Holman's Lewes Directory.*

*Above: The school's closure is
recorded in 1882. 'Right Hon.
the Speaker' was Viscount
Hampden at Glynde, then
the Speaker of the House of
Commons*

*Below: The 1887 entry for
the Lewes Exhibition Fund*

Public Schools.

GRAMMAR SCHOOL, ST. ANN'S.

Built about 1714. The original School was founded in Southover by Mrs. Agnes Morley 200 years before, who left an annuity to be laid out in salaries for the master and usher, and in repairs of the premises. The management of the School is vested in Trustees, who have the nomination of the schoolmaster. According to the instructions of the Foundress, the schoolmaster is to be a priest capable of teaching grammar. He is not to give up the School without one year's warning to the Trustees, nor to have the care of souls or any other impediment to his attention to the School, and he is not to have anything of the parents or friends of the scholars, except they give him of their own benevolence. Mrs. Mary Jenkins, in 1706, gave £1000 to purchase lands for the use and benefit of the School. A part of this money was appropriated in building the present School-house; The transfer of the School from Southover to St. Ann taking place about 1714. The remainder of the money was laid out so as to bring in an annual sum of £35 a year. Mr. Thos. Blunt also made a bequest to the School in the year 1611 of £3 a year.

TRUSTEES :

Right Hon. the Earl of Chichester.
Right Hon. Lord Viscount Gage.
Lord Pelham.
W. L. Christie, Esq., M.P.
Geo. Molineux, Esq.
Robt. Crosskey, Esq.
E. C. Currey, Esq.
M. S. Blaker, Esq.
R. Turner, Esq.

Right Hon. the Speaker, G.C.B.
Right Hon. J. G. Dodson, M.P.
Rev. Sir G. C. Shiffner, Bart.
J. G. Blencowe, Esq.
J. H. Sclater, Esq.
Geo. Whitfeld, Esq.
J. C. Lucas, Esq.
G. C. Rigden, Esq.
F. Verrall, Esq.

The School is closed at present, pending an alteration or re-construction in its Management.

LEWES EXHIBITION FUND.

Governors :

J. G. Blencowe, Esq.
E. C. Currey, Esq.
R. Crosskey, Esq.
J. C. Lucas, Esq.,

R. Turner, Esq.,
W. E. Baxter, Esq.
Alderman C. R. Kemp.
Alderman T. Parsons.

And the Mayor for the time being.

Chairman of Governors : E. C. Currey, Esq.

Clerk to Governors : Mr. J. West, 6, Grange Road, Lewes.

Regulations :

The Trusts and Endowments of the late Grammar School, Blunt's Charity and Steere's Exhibition having been consolidated into one Foundation under the above title and New Trusts declared in a scheme of the Charity Commissioners confirmed by Order in Council, the Governors appointed under the scheme hereby issue the following Regulations for carrying its provisions into effect :—

1.—There shall be maintained, so far as the Fund for the time being may permit, the following Exhibitions :—namely, One Exhibition of the annual value of £20, Ten of the annual value of £12 each, and Eight of the annual value of £6 each, to be awarded to children of persons resident in the Municipal Borough of Lewes, or within five miles of the County Hall.

2.—The first-named Exhibition shall be competed for in such manner as the Governors may from time to time direct. The Holder shall be or become a Student at one of the Universities of Oxford or Cambridge, and be entitled to enjoy the same for four years, provided he or she so long continue a Resident Member of the University.

3.—The other Exhibitions shall, as far as possible, be awarded equally between boys and girls. These Exhibitions shall be tenable for four years at places of education higher than Elementary (schools in Lewes having the preference) to be selected by the Exhibitioners, subject to the approval of the Governors.

Private Passions

Thomas Reader White in his mayor's regalia. He took over the school in 1883.

THE MAN WHO TOOK the plunge and saved Lewes Grammar School had one invaluable asset: experience. Thomas Reader White, a town councillor and future mayor, had previously run a commercial school in the Cliffe for many years, and when disaster befell the ancient institution at the top of the hill, he was quick to seize the opportunity.

On January 20th 1883 the trustees (still in control pending the establishment of the new exhibition fund) resolved 'to endeavour' to let the premises on a repairing lease. Exactly a month later White offered to take the premises on a 21-year lease at £105 a year, finally settling for £110 after being assured that the drainage would be repaired first.

Holman's Lewes Directory for that year reported that 'The school, having been closed for some time, has been put into thorough repair, and is now leased by the trustees to Mr T.R. White, formerly of Cliffe House. A recreation ground has been secured for the use of the pupils.'

White was employing D.E. Wright, B.A., Queen's College, Cambridge, as his assistant classical and mathematical master, James Meredith as assistant master and Jules Lewy B.A. as 'professor of French'. Two years later the master was the Rev Charles Kevern Williams MA, 'late fellow of Pembroke College, Oxford', which suggests that White was determined to restore the school's reputation for classical scholarship.

Although the name was retained, however, it had a genteel prefix in *Kelly's Directory*: 'Young gentlemen's boarding school, Grammar School, High Street.'

For glimpses of events over the next twenty years and more we have to peer through the narrow keyhole of the exhibition fund minutes. Its governors were necessarily concerned primarily with the state of the building and the rent they took from it, rather than the education practised within its walls. We may assume that White ran his school efficiently, as he remained at the helm for all of ten years, but (rent aside) he features only when, in 1894, the National Telephone Company has 'placed an

Floreat Lewys

1893
*Keir Hardie forms
Independent Labour Party*

1899–1902
Boer War

1901–1910
Reign of Edward VII

erection upon the Grammar School without any permission of the Governors', and White is asked to have the offending telegraph pole removed.

By this time, although legally the leaseholder, he was no longer the headmaster. In 1893 he had passed the baton to the Rev Henry Cruickshank, a man who turned out to have rather less staying power, leaving after less than three years. He had been warden of St Kenelm's College in Brighton and (for only a brief period, thank goodness) he changed the name of his Lewes school to St Kenelm's College, too.

The grammar school, c. 1890, under Thomas Reader White. The photograph was taken in Shelleys car park, and all the names are written on the back.

Standing (left to right): Mr Clinch (master), S. Elphick, E. King, H. Waddington, J. Floyd, H. Hall, T.R. White (headmaster), R. Hall, Jos Langridge, Mrs White, Mr Pearce (master), G.C. Broadbent, H.V. Fuller, D. Thompson, H.B. Cook, T.S. Wilkinson, H. Allwork, L. Vinall, J.C. Lucas, G.J.R. Uridge, M. Stacey, P. Card, French pupil.

Sitting: H. Reed, R. James, P.H. Vinall, N.E. Bannister, A.T. Langridge, M. Broad, J. Cox, G.A. Broad, W.M. Pannett, G. Vinall, F. Barratt, A. Massingham, G. Cox, E. Harris, G. Watson, F.J. Hodson, W. Hodson, T.C. Saxby, B. Whiteman, H. Wilson, L Sydney, N. Madgwick.

His successor, the Rev Edward Hodgson, began in expansive mood, for soon after he arrived he was given permission to erect an 'iron chapel' in the school playground – presumably at his own expense. We can imagine him proudly ringing the ship's bell he installed there to summon the boys to services.

Subsquent events reveal, however, that both Cruickshank and Hodgson suffered serious money worries. There's no reason to doubt the passion for education which moved these men to tackle what, with hindsight, seems to have been a hopeless task. Indeed, their enthusiasm for it may have blinded them to the harsh realities.

The governors had reduced the rent from £110 to £90 a year for Hodgson, but when his lease came up for renewal in 1904 they refused his request to cut it still further. Their reply that they would agree to £100 a year 'provided an approved guarantee can be found for punctual payment' speaks volumes.

In January 1905 Hodgson sold the school to Charles Shepherd Smith, who paid a thousand pounds by way of goodwill. At his bankruptcy hearing years later, Shepherd Smith would be asked why he had stumped up so much.

'I don't know,' he replied, adding sadly, 'We have been living in a fool's paradise.'

We can follow the crumbling of Shepherd Smith's dream through the minutes of the exhibition fund. His best year, he was later to say, was 1909, but by the end of 1911 he was in arrears with his rent by more than a year. The following February he asked the governors time to pay on the promise of clearing some of his debt, and in the September he was hoping they might grant him a new lease at a lower rent. Better terms were later granted, but only on the condition that he put down a £10 deposit and paid off all his arrears 'forthwith' – something he was clearly unable to do.

Plans prepared by Powell & Co for Hodgson's iron chapel. It also served as a lecture room and was later converted into a chemistry lab. [ESRO]

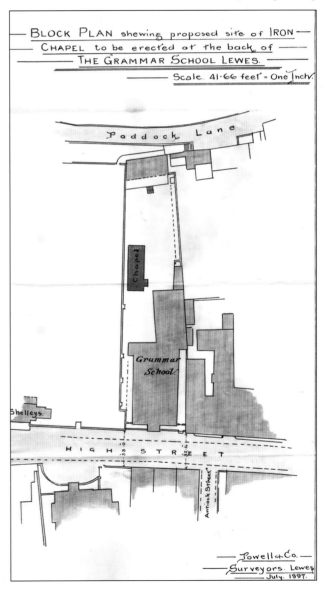

BLOCK PLAN shewing proposed site of IRON CHAPEL to be erected at the back of THE GRAMMAR SCHOOL LEWES.

Scale. 41·66 feet = One Inch.

Paddock Lane

Chapel

Grammar School

Shelleys.

HIGH STREET

Antиck Street

Powell & Co.
Surveyors. Lewes
July. 1897.

George Holman, who praised Shepherd Smith, was seven times mayor of Lewes between 1898 and 1911

MYSTERY MAN 1

In May 1911 Charles Shepherd Smith asked permission to share the lease of the school with W. Wynne Hall.

The following March Hall's name appears directly under Shepherd Smith's in the list of thirty people (*page 63*) calling for a public meeting to consider the school's re-constitution.

Was he proposing to go into partnership with the headmaster? If so, he presumably got cold feet: he is not mentioned again in the exhibition fund minutes.

Architect's drawing of the iron chapel. [ESRO]

TOWN PRIDE

Dire as the situation had become, nobody seems to have blamed the headmaster or his predecessor. At one of several meetings called to discuss the school's future, seven-times mayor George Holman – to cries of 'hear! hear!' – went out of his way to praise Shepherd Smith, who had 'waged a very uphill fight during the last few years to get the school into its present satisfactory state'.

What everyone knew was that the world of education was changing fast, and that Lewes was being left behind. There were grammar schools in Brighton and Uckfield where bright lads could get a good education subsidised by the state. Worse, the Lewes Exhibition Fund gave scholarships to local children who were being taught outside the borough. 'It's true that I have had one or two of them,' Shepherd Smith said, 'but others are held at the Brighton grammar school and all over the place.'

If Lewes was to punch its weight as the county town it needed to offer quality secondary education, and the school's 400th anniversary saw an energetic campaign to put it back where many felt it belonged. At a public meeting on March 26th, 1912, a proposal was made to recover the endowments which, thirty years before, the charity commissioners had decided should be transferred to the exhibition fund.

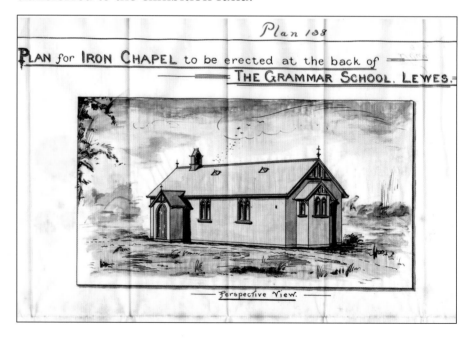

Plan 138

PLAN for IRON CHAPEL to be erected at the back of THE GRAMMAR SCHOOL, LEWES.

Perspective View.

	Back Row	4th Row	3rd Row	2nd Row	Front Row
	Lewes Old Grammar School		1899		
1	Henry	S. St John Smith	Parsons	Griffiths	P. Chevens
2	G. Broad	?	?	Wilmshurst	S. Langridge
3	Burns	Massingham	?	?	?
4	Lewin	L. Martin	?	?	?
5	Stone	?	Woods	?	Savage
6	Rosser	Maclaren	Mrs Hodgson	?	S. Fuller
7	D. Berry	G. Lloyd	Rev. Hodgson (Headmaster)	E. C. Russell	?
8	Stafford	F. A. Russell	Hammans	S. C. Lloyd	?
9	S. Vine	B. Bruce	Casey (music)	—	Caröll
10	?	Cheetham	Maclaren	B. Conlan	?
11	?	Cheal	?	Hughes	Watson
12	R. Stone	C. T. Lloyd	Haydon	?	T. Cox
13	?	Moon	—	?	L. Stone
14	—	Horwood	—	—	?
15	—	?	—	—	Carvill
16	—	Barron	—	—	Groves
17	—	Gaster	—		—
18	—	Pitman	—		
19	—	?			

Rev Edward Hodgson (bearded, middle of centre row) with his wife, staff and pupils in 1899. He had taken over the school on the first day of 1896.

GOOD NEIGHBOURS

The Busby family, who lived next door to the school in the 1890s, encouraged the boys at their cricket by placing a sixpence on the stumps. It was a reward for the bowler whose accuracy managed to dislodge it.

1901
Electricity supply comes to Lewes

1902
First old age pension

1906
Liberals win landslide election

1910–1936
Reign of George V

1910
Lewes Victoria Hospital opens

1912
Titanic disaster; Captain Scott dies on Antarctic expedition

A poster advising ratepayers of a meeting in March 1912 to discuss the reconstitution of the grammar school. [ESRO]

A 'reconstruction committee' was formed, led by the Rev Robert Belcher. A deputation travelled to Whitehall, where it received an unsympathetic response from Dr R.P. Scott at the Board of Education. The Board, he told them, not only declined to take any steps without the approval of the exhibition fund and the local education authority, but the financial proposals 'could not be justified', a suitable playing field was required as a condition of recognition and the building wasn't up to scratch.

In the case of old grammar schools which had not ceased to be charitable foundations, he said, the Board did not always insist upon modern building regulations being observed, but 'no such relaxation could be allowed in the present case owing to the break in the continuity of the school'.

Undaunted, the committee submitted a memorandum to the East Sussex education committee and the governors of the exhibition fund. It looked back to that earlier period when the school fell out of favour.

'In 1881 public secondary education was at a low ebb, and in particular local authorities were not as a rule responsible for it. Today, with the support of government grant and rate aid, and with the resumption of the old endowments, efficiency may be attained without any heavy charge on the rates.'

It spoke about 'the patriotism of the district', but added that the school would be unable to continue without change.

The Brighton run

Several speakers at the public meeting said it was wrong that boys should have to travel to Brighton for their education. The *Sussex Express* reported the words of Councillor Lloyd, who remembered the nuisance they had caused other passengers in days gone by.

'When passing through Falmer tunnel boys used to leave their carriage, walk along the footboard and put their heads into other carriages and frighten the occupants, while it was not unusual for a lighted squib to be thrown into other carriages.'

'Most of the pupils are the sons of parents of very modest means, and the school is placed in competition with public secondary schools in Brighton and elsewhere which, being aided by government grants and rates, in addition to endowments, are in a position to provide more complete educational advantages at a lower fee.'

It threw in a few facts and figures for good measure:

- *Uckfield Grammar school, supported by the East Sussex education authority, had tuition fees of £6 and £8 a year, whereas the Lewes figure was £12*

- *Brighton's municipal secondary school had admitted Lewes boys for £4 14s 6d a year, but next year this would rise to £7 17s 6d, with Lewes boys admitted only if no Brighton pupils were available*

The committee and Shepherd Smith seem to have overstated the drain on Lewes youth to the surrounding area, since figures released by the Exhibition Fund itself showed that it currently had 38 exhibitioners (equally divided between boys and girls) with nine boys at the grammar school, six at Castlegate School in Lewes, two at the grammar school at Brighton and one at Brighton Technical College. Although the campaigners made great play of the fact that some were 'as far away as Littlehampton and Taunton' (a girl and boy respectively), these seemingly perverse postings were simply the result of family moves after the awards had been made.

But the exhibition fund wasn't the problem. Its governors had recently been rapped over the knuckles by the Board of Education, which had stressed the importance of sending its exhibitioners to 'a recognised secondary school', and they must have realised what that would mean for Lewes. They quickly pronounced in favour of the scheme, while emphasising that half of their funds were earmarked for girls and one exhibition specifically for a university place.

It was East Sussex County Council that refused to budge, despite the striking fact that it was about to open (in 1913) a girls' grammar school in the town. Its education committee decided

---

COME AND JOIN US

Through all the trials of Shepherd Smith's last years the school took out a regular advertisement in the *Sussex Express*.

In keeping with its former high standing it mentioned its 1512 founding date and proclaimed its 'visitors' to be 'The Lord Bishop of Chichester' and 'The Most Noble the Marquis of Abergavenny', but it stressed that the school gave both a classical and a modern education.

It offered 'successful preparation for local exams and BUSINESS, shorthand, German, book-keeping, drawing etc.'

There was also a preparatory department for younger boys, with individual attention and 'careful grounding'.

1913

Founding of Lewes County Grammar School for Girls

Notice of a meeting in May 1913 at which the committee reported the failure of its attempt to restore the fortunes of the grammar school. The Sussex Express *reported that a 'vigilante committee' would remain in place, 'and it is hoped the time is not far distant when their labours will be attended with greater success.' [ESRO]*

on straightforward financial grounds that its commitment to the boys' grammar schools in Brighton, Uckfield and Rye prevented their involvement with another one.

This brought a tart response from Belcher's committee.

> Those responsible for the provision of educational facilities often complain of the lack of public interest in educative work, but if when the public display an interest in such a work their proposals are treated as the proposals of the committee have been, the explanation of the lack of interest is not far to seek.
>
> The attitude of the Board of Education was distinctly hostile to the proposals of your committee, and suggested that any scheme for a new school was a fit subject for adverse criticism rather than for a careful and favourable consideration.
>
> The East Sussex Education Committee, after inviting the submission of more definite proposals, refused to confer with the committee on those proposals, giving no reaon for this refusal, and the committee wish to place on record their surprise that the local education authority for secondary education should not be willing at least to discuss a scheme such as that which was put forward.

NOTHING LEFT

It was the previous April, the 40-year-old Shepherd Smith told his bankruptcy hearing in November 1913, that he had realised 'all was up'. (The committee officially conceded defeat in May). 'But I don't pretend to deny,' he added, 'that for a long time before that I had difficulty in paying my way.'

Newspaper accounts of the headmaster's financial collapse make uncomfortable reading. He appeared at county hall before the registrar, Montague Baker, and the official receiver, Thomas Gourlay. First the brutal realites were itemised:

Excess of liabilities over assets	£763 2s 0d
Estimated loss in carrying on school from November 3, 1912 until date of receivership order	£450 0s 0d
Bad debts	£39 17s 7d
Personal expenses of wife and four children since 3/11/1912	£200 0s 0d

Lewes Prep. School 1909 . J R R in light suit . At least 1/3 killed 1914–18

Shepherd Smith's school. The faded writing on the card frame reads, 'Lewes Prep School 1909 J R R in light suit At least 1/3 killed 1914–1918.' A sketch key on the reverse chiefly refers to those standing behind the rail and those perched on the low wall in front of it, with question marks for several of them. Note the presence of Rev Evan Griffiths, who would later take over the school. There seem to have been two Martel brothers. Although the Grammar School name remained the official title, most pupils were now in the lower age range.

Behind rail: ? Martel, Martel d 1914–18 Rev Griffiths ? Mr & Mrs Shepherd Smith ? ? Palmer, Bill Rich

Sitting on the wall: Lee Haydon d. 1914–18 ? Eric Skinner d. 1914–18 ? Yates d. 1914–18 Wilmshurst (Ringmer) d. 1914–18, Wyborn.

A further note reads, 'Farmer Lee (Fulking) on right of group. Jed Marsh behind him.'

1914–1918
First world war

1915
Lewes Western Road School (Mixed) is first county school in Lewes for 9–12 age range

---

FULL TO BURSTING

Volunteers for the first world war were billeted in Lewes in prodigious numbers, as recorded in the memoirs of George Holman, the first freeman of the borough:

'Over 12,000 men were dumped into the town in less than 48 hours. Trains were constantly arriving, day and night, packed with men from the mining and other districts, some of them taken straight from the pits in working garb, to be billeted in every part of the town.

'The normal population was suddenly doubled, and every house had to share the responsibility of the sudden invasion.

'The town hall, parish rooms, old workhouse, Corn Exchange and every available shelter was occupied.'

He told the court that he had come to the school in January, 1905; that his tenancy cost him £85 a year plus £51 a year for an adjoining field; that he owed money to a range of local traders; and that he had been in debt to money-lenders since December 1911. In 1909, 'when Lord Gage gave away the prizes', he had 80 boys, some 26 of them boarders, but those figures had recently come down to about 45 and 13 respectively. He thought that he had made a profit in his best years, but agreed with the receiver that this did not constitute a 'living profit'.

Gourlay now painstakingly explored his downfall.

'I understand this school has had rather a disastrous history altogether, of late at any rate?'
'Yes.'
'Have the two previous masters there both become involved in financial difficulties?'
'Yes.'
'One of them became a bankrupt and the other had to arrange with the creditors?'
'Yes.'
'As a matter of fact, was he not arranging with them when you bought the school?'
'Yes.'
'Under these circumstances, what induced you to give a price like £1,000 for it?'
'I don't know. We wanted a school and thought there were possibilities in the place.'
'It was too much?'
'Yes . . . We have been living in a fool's paradise.'

The receiver then enquired about what it was that Shepherd Smith had bought for his thousand pounds.

'Did it include anything that is not there still?'
'No.'
'We have got it all?'
'It included goodwill.'
'Is that there still?'
'I am afraid not.' [*Laughter*]
'Do you think a school can be conducted successfully in Lewes under present conditions?'
'Not under present conditions. I must reluctantly say not.'

MILITARY INTERVENTION

The school was now closed (the recruiting agency Gabbitas and Thring offered to advertise for a new tenant), but the campaigners refused to lie down. At yet another public meeting they proposed a fresh idea: forget the existing grammar school and ask the county council to create a completely new one. Although new classrooms and labs would be needed elsewhere, one alderman said, 'the present grammar school buildings would do for the master's residence and for boarders'.

Such faint hopes as they may have had were soon dashed by a catastrophe compared with which the school's miseries were a triviality. On August 4th 1914 Britain entered the first world war. The school building was ideal as a barracks, and before long a large contingent of Canadian soldiers had taken up occupation. A sentry with fixed bayonet would march up and down outside.

In 1915 the Dudeney family next door had complained of damp from the grammar school affecting their property, and the history of Canadian army occupation suggests that the place would have needed a fair amount of care and attention when they left early the following year. The governors' minutes that May reported their hope of finding someone to look after the premises while they were unlet, and it must have been with some relief that Henry Wansey (*panel, right*) was prepared to take it on for a rent of £25 a year that August.

Grammar School   Lewes.

MYSTERY MAN 2

In January 1916 the exhibition fund governors received a letter from Rev H. Raymond Wansey, asking how much it would cost to rent the grammar school.

The 42-year old had recently returned from Japan with his wife and five children, having worked for the Church Missionary Society there.

In August 1916 he took a lease on the schoolroom, playground and ground floor. A year later he was gone.

Wansey in Japan.

Early postcard view of the school.

A HORRIBLE DIN

Someone at the grammar school was fond of hammering away at the piano, to the distraction of the neighbours.

'Poor E[rnest] driven raving mad by that fool at the piano over the way,' Mrs Dudeney writes with typical abruptness in October 1919. 'I went & asked Mrs Reid if her lodger complained so that we might make a joint complaint. Unfortunately her lodger is deaf.

'Strumming so abominable that I went across the road to complain. Found it came from Griffiths next door!'

Three days later she writes: 'I spoke to Griffiths about the infernal noise on the piano & he very nicely promised to put a stop to it.'

She went for a soldier

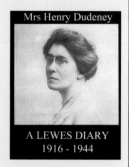

Mrs Henry Dudeney

A LEWES DIARY
1916 - 1944

'**A**t midday, horrid shock,' reads the first entry in Mrs Henry Dudeney's 1916 diary. 'Letter from Lock Hospital saying Bessie G. going to have a baby. I must "remove" her.'

Mrs Dudeney, then a famous novelist, lived next door to the school at 138 High Street with her husband Henry. (For her he was Ernest, his middle name. 'Bessie' was her servant Elizabeth.)

In a later entry she would recall 'the soldiers at the grammar school calling out of the window to Bessie in the yard on Christmas morning, "Got the pudding in, Cookey?"' Now she wrote: 'Poor Elizabeth, the 150 soldiers at the grammar school were her undoing. And shall I ever forget that day when I took her to the Lock Hospital.'

Bessie had been sent to hospital because of another condition, which meant that Mrs Dudeney had *two* pieces of bad news to impart to her family.

January 7: 'Wrote to her mother in Devonshire (who had written to me asking what was the matter with Bessie). I told her the truth as gently as I could: venereal disease and going to have a baby.'

A Canadian soldier on guard outside the school.

It didn't take Wansey long to discover what a daunting prospect this was. By the following February he had written to the governors asking for financial support in carrying on his school, but they replied that they had no funds available.

THE GRIFFITHS ERA

At this lowest ebb in its fortunes, the school found a new saviour in the Rev Canon Evan Griffiths. His presence in the photograph of Shepherd Smith's school (*page 67*) suggests a long involvement with it, and in May 1917 he wrote to the exhibition fund applying for the tenancy. The governors' minutes show that Wansey wanted to stay should they fail to grant a lease to Griffiths – which indicates that the local man was the preferred candidate.

The governors came to an agreement with him the following month. Their first proposal was to put the building in order with the exception of the large schoolroom and the dormitories over the top of it, but Griffiths persuaded them not only to include the schoolroom in the repairs but to strip the external brickwork of its *ampelopsis* – the once-fashionable climbing vine that shrouded so many buildings at that period.

MIND GAMES

Mrs Dudeney's husband, Henry (*above*), had his own claim to fame as the 'Puzzle King', sending brain-teasers to national magazines – and he regularly pitted his wits against Evan Griffiths over the chess board.

An entry in the diary for March 1919 reads 'At night Mr Griffiths played chess with E. & rather exhausted him.'

She evidently regarded these visits as somewhat relentless, for she writes in February 1922: 'Mr Griffiths didn't come! For a wonder.'

The grammar school clothed in ampelopsis. *Griffiths had it removed.*

1916
February
Battle of Verdun
July
Battle of the Somme

1917
April
Battle of Vimy Ridge
July
*Third battle of Ypres
(Passchendaele)*

1918
July
Second Battle of the Marne
November 11
Germany signs armistice

War memorial, School Hill

At the same time the governors did a deal with Shelley's. The hotel would reduce the height of the dividing wall, while the exhibition fund recognised that a long-disputed strip of land to the west of the school belonged to the hotel.

We can only imagine the underlying emotions when Canon Griffiths re-opened for business in September 1917. Many of the youngsters he had known at Shepherd Smith's school had, on reaching their very young manhood, answered Lord Kitchener's call to fight in that 'war to end all wars'. Many were dead, others were missing and still the fighting continued. Not a few of the lads who now grouped around him must have been from those same families, and scarcely a single one of them would have been untouched by the slaughter in one grim way or another.

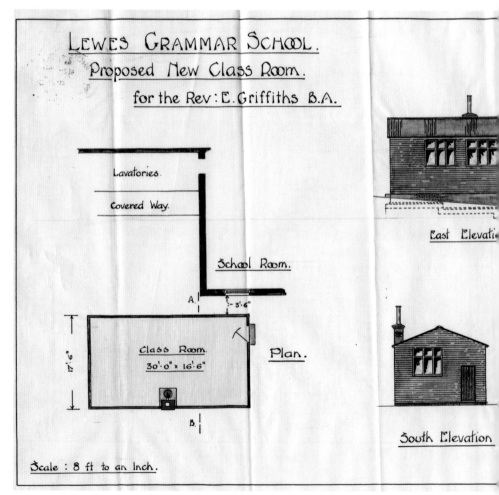

Griffiths seems to have had the magic touch: he became a fixture, running the grammar school for the next fifteen years. By the October of 1922 his numbers had swollen sufficiently for him to request that the premises be extended. The governors replied that they couldn't afford anything so ambitious, but that they were prepared to allow the erection of a temporary building 'subject to his first submitting a plan of the proposed building for their approval and to his giving an undertaking to remove the building at the end of his tenancy and reinstate the ground to its present condition'.

The plans (*below*) were approved the following year, and we can see that it's on the same spot as Edward Hodgson's former chapel. Perhaps that had reached the end of its useful life.

Canon Griffiths

The school cleared of its vegetation.

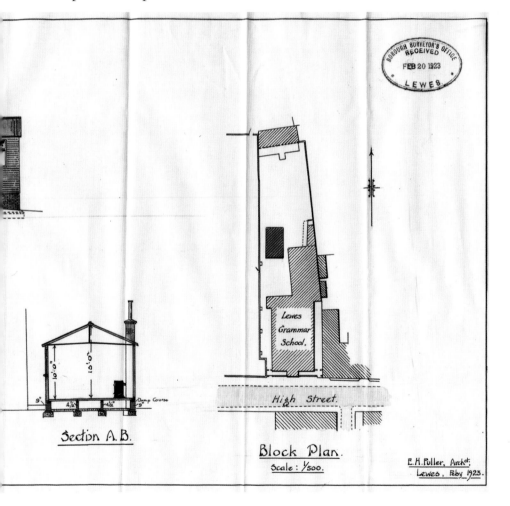

Plans for Rev Griffiths' new classroom, prepared by the Lewest architect Ernest Fuller in 1923. [ESRO]

1920
Wynne Baxter gives Pells to the town

1924
First Labour government, under Ramsay MacDonald

1929
Wall Street Crash begins the Depression

1930
Lewes County Grammar School for Boys founded

Canon Griffiths and his school in 1921.

In July 1932 Griffiths wrote to the exhibition fund asking whether he could buy the building, but the governors' minutes reveal that he was in too much of a hurry. They were not, they said, prepared to make a decision 'in such a short time as mentioned in his letter', but 'in the event of his succeeding in finding a suitable purchaser of the goodwill of the school, the governors would be prepared to grant a lease for a term not exceeding 21 years at a rental of £100 per annum'.

Why the rush? Griffiths had evidently already decided to step down. That Easter the parishes of St Thomas and All Saints had been combined, and he now found himself rector of both, as well as rural dean for the Lewes area – a considerable workload. Perhaps, too, he felt that the recent opening of a new county grammar school for boys in the town, under its charismatic first head Neville Bradshaw, had rendered his provision for the older boys superfluous. The school would surely be a more attractive proposition to a prospective buyer if it included the premises – and that buyer was probably already waiting in the wings. For Canon Griffiths, alas, trouble was in store.

THE GRAMMAR SCHOOL
·OCTOBER *(*

THE EBULLIENT MR VAUGHAN

The dean was, of course, highly respected in Lewes, and he would himself later serve on the board of the exhibition fund, but a note from a governors' meeting on December 19th 1932 expresses their undisguised displeasure:

> The attention of the governors being drawn to the fact that the Revd E. Griffiths had either sublet or assigned his tenancy of the grammar school to a Mr Vaughan, who was now in occupation of the premises, and that the quarter's rent due at Michaelmas last was still outstanding, the clerk was directed to write to the Revd E. Griffiths pressing for payment of the rent without further delay, and to inform him that the governors did not recognise Mr Vaughan's occupancy in any shape or form, and that they still looked to him (Mr Griffiths) as their tenant.

Did the governors know something that Griffiths didn't? And, if so, what would they have made of the effusive back-slapping and grandiose speech-making during the school's Christmas celebrations the very next day?

An advertisement for the school in Kelly's Blue Book for 1931–1932.

LEWES, SUSSEX
1921

Photo by PANORA, LTD., 56-58 Eagle Street, London, W.C.1.

MYSTERY MAN 3

David Vaughan is another of those characters who play a fleeting, but intriguing, role in the grammar school story.

In his Christmas speech he spoke of his belief in the youth of the day, saying that he had no sympathy with those who condemned them as shallow and rude.

'His experience taught him,' the *Sussex Express* reported, 'that children today were nicer than children used to be.

'They were, perhaps, more outspoken, but they were certainly loyal, sincere and generally clean-minded, preferrng good to evil, but they wanted guidance towards the good.'

Were his ambitious plans for the school the fantasies of a plausible con-man, or was he undone by a catastrophe not of his own making? We shall probably never know .

He seems to have arrived out of nowhere in a blaze of good intentions, vanishing just as quickly without leaving a trace behind.

The *Sussex Express* reported the festivities with enthusiasm. First there was an afternoon party in the large school hall, at which '75 guests did justice to a wonderful supply of dainties' before 'Barnard, on behalf of the sixth form, presented a piece of silver to Mrs Vaughan, with an expression of their good wishes'.

This was followed by an evening concert of music and drama at the Corn Exchange, in which all the school performed, from the preparatory form (which 'portrayed in song and action the old story of the Ten Little Nigger Boys') to Mrs Vaughan herself – 'a singer of taste and experience' who gave 'a delightful rendering of Braid the Raven Hair (from the Mikado) and Coming Through the Rye.'

But the serious business was the retirement of the long-serving headmaster and the coronation of his successor. Not only had David E. Vaughan B.A. taken up residence at the school, but he had been running it since the retirement of Evan Griffiths in September. The Rev Griffiths was presented with a gold wrist watch and his wife with a silver tea service.

The stage was set for a stirring speech by Vaughan, who said he could 'only aim at making myself a worthy successor to a worthy man'. He thanked everyone who had made his first term in Lewes such a happy one, and he included in that number Messrs Every of the Phoenix Ironworks, without explaining what 'their kindness in many ways' amounted to.

Educationally, he said, the school continued to be a success, with Curtis and Thomson Minor picking up two of the five exhibition fund scholarships. As for the future, he had a host of new initiatives to announce:

- *A new gymnasium would be in use in the New Year*
- *The art class was to be 'augmented'*
- *A science laboratory would be opened 'if possible'*
- *An Old Boys Association was to be formed, with an initial target of 300 members*
- *A new school magazine would be published next term, a section of it devoted to the Old Boys*

Canon Griffiths must have stepped down with the sense of a job well done, while for the boys and their parents Christmas had surely come a few days early.

Fast-forward a month to the next governors' meeting on January 27th 1933, and we find a surprising minute.

> A letter from the Revd E. Griffiths dated 22 December last, asking whether the governors were prepared to grant a lease of the grammar school to Mr Vaughan, who was now in occupation of the premises, was read and considered.
>
> Resolved that a reply be sent to the Revd E. Griffiths pointing out the change of circumstances in connection with Mr Vaughan's occupancy which had taken place since the date of his (Mr Griffiths) letter, and to enquire what action he now proposed to take in consequence of such change.

David Vaughan had gone! Why and where we unfortunately cannot say, but there can be little doubt that Evan Griffiths had a large amount of egg on his face. He couldn't afford to make the same mistake twice.

THE LEWIS ERA

A peppery, energetic Welshman now stepped into the breach. The Rev Cecil Lewis initially took only a three-year lease on the building in 1933, but he would carry the school forward for more than three decades – from the years of the Great Depression, through a second world war and (although we can't imagine that he had the slightest enthusiasm for it) into the hang-loose social revolution of the Swinging Sixties.

What kind of a school did he run? There were, inevitably, some changes during the long period of his headship, but one thing he never attempted to do was compete with the state school in Mountfield Road, which had much better resources. His was primarily a 'prep' school, taking pupils at the age of five and preparing them for secondary schooling elsewhere, with only the less academically gifted staying on with him until they were eighteen.

He taught girl pupils alongside the boys during the war years, gradually phased them out afterwards and then ran mixed classes once again when the PNEU girls' school in Southover

---

A WORSHIPFUL
BROTHER

Canon Griffiths signed off from the school with a toast he had made every year: 'A very happy Christmas, a prosperous New Year to all – and plenty of plum pudding!'

Although still busy with his clerical duties, he was able to devote more time to his other interests once he stepped down from the school.

One of them was freemasonry. Between 1933 and 1938 he edited six booklets recording the transactions of the Sussex Masters Lodge no. 3672, based in Brighton.

His masonic title was Worshipful Brother, which indicates that he was a former Master of the lodge.

1936
Reign and abdication of Edward VIII

1936–1952
Reign of George VI

1939–45
Second world war

1940
Food rationing begins

1943 January 20th
'Lewes Blitz': six bombs dropped, killing two and seriously injuring eleven

1944
Butler Education Act introduces tripartite system for secondary education (grammar, secondary modern and technical schools) and makes secondary education free for all pupils

1945
Clement Attlee heads post-war Labour government

1948
National Health Service created

1951
Festival of Britain; Tories elected under Winston Churchill

The old-fashioned classrooms were unchanged during the headship of Cecil Lewis.

closed down in the 1950s. As for boarding, he still lodged some two dozen lads in the early 50s (some termly; most of them by the week), but this practice was about to end. While the boys were in residence he lived out, but once their dormitories had been closed he and his family – a younger second wife, Nancy,

LEWES GRAMMAR SCHOOL. THE SCHOOL HALL.

LEWES GRAMMAR SCHOOL. PREPARATORY ROOM.

and their daughter Ann (*see pages 86–87*) – moved into the upstairs rooms at the school.

What changed very little was the antiquated atmosphere of the classrooms. The photographs on the facing page have an ancient look to them, but Lewis saw no reason to update the interior, and the teaching environment when he left was just as he had first found it.

A HOME OF OUR OWN

His lasting legacy to future generations was the building itself. Ever since Thomas Reader White took over the school in 1883, its masters had rented it from the Lewes Exhibition Fund. In 1932 Evan Griffiths had had his offer to buy it rebuffed, but in May 1951 Cecil Lewis decided to try again.

The first response from the governors was encouraging. They asked the Ministry of Education – which had long since taken over responsibility from the Charity Commission – whether the government was prepared to allow the sale 'in consequence of the age of the building and the inability of the governors to finance the cost of adapting it to meet the requirements of the ministry'.

A game of cat-and-mouse ensued. Lewis offered £2,000 and warned that he would be looking for a 45-year lease should there be no sale. The governors put a £3,500 tag on it, which prompted the headmaster to say that he was no longer interested.

In November a new bidder appeared on the scene: 'Mr L.D.A. Cowan M.A.' was prepared to buy the freehold for £3,500. The only word from Lewis at this time was a letter complaining of 'the nuisance arising from the overhanging trees in the adjoining Shelleys property' – he had a running feud with the owner, and the pair would sometimes stage shouting matches in the area between the two buildings.

The ministry expressed itself happy with a sale, but perhaps asked the exhibition fund to think again about the price. By March 1952 Cowan had increased his offer to all of £5,025. The governors, playing the field, now wrote to Lewis to ask whether he was prepared to go beyond this and to let them have an answer by September 29th.

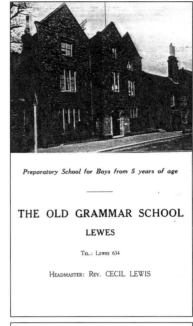

Press advertisement for the school in the late 1950s.

"Shelleys Hotel had a cockatoo which lived in their entrance hall. It used to fly out into the street, and we'd watch it through the window."

"On Sunday mornings the boarders went to the service at St John's church in Southover, and we were each given a penny to put in the collection bag."

"We had exactly the same menu every week. It wasn't very good, and I hated stew on Tuesdays because there was always a lot of gristle in the meat."

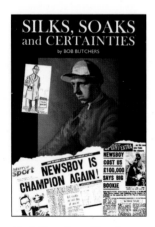

Bob Butchers' book.

Cowan's agents, perhaps fearing the worst, tried the heavy-handed approach and were gently held at arm's length: 'Whilst sympathising with the object mentioned in their letter,' a fund minute reads, 'the governors did not see their way to serve a notice to quit on Mr Lewis during the course of the negotiations.'

Their clerk was in fact authorised to serve such a notice on Lewis if he failed to respond by the 29th, but the headmaster (who seems to have played his hand with the skill of a practised poker player) immediately upped his offer to £5,175 and was awarded the freehold. From this time forward the school and its building were one.

FROM THE HORSE'S MOUTH

We now enter the period of living memory, and can at last form a personal picture of day-to-day life at the school. The building, as we have seen, was little changed from decades before. The boys entered under the arch to the left of the main entrance, nearest Shelleys, and the girls to the right. Corporal punishment was commonplace (Lewis had a collection of canes, from thin and whippy to heavy), but not excessively so for the time.

The standard of education seems to have been adequate rather than high-flying, although John Hecks – now in his nineties and taught successively under Canon Griffiths, David Vaughan and Cecil Lewis – remembers 'a very good school' with Lewis 'popular and pleasant – greatly respected.'

Bob Butchers was among Cecil Lewis's first fresh intake in 1933. Born into a racing family, he was determined on a career involving horses, became the original Newsboy tipster for the *Daily Mirror* (he stayed for almost 39 years) and later published his colourful memoirs under the title *Silks, Soaks and Certainties*.

'It seemed a fair standard of education,' to me, he recalls nearly eighty years on, 'but we weren't judged by exams in those days. I went to the secondary school without having to take one.

'Discipline was fairly strict, and you'd get a reprimand if you were caught out of school without a cap on. At the school bell you had to form ranks according to the class you were in, and the Rev Lewis would appear and bellow 'Shun, right turn, march!' – not much different from the army.

Cecil Lewis took over the school in 1933, and this is one of his first Christmas parties. He can be seen beaming in the corner, wearing his dog collar, while his first wife sits opposite him (second from left), flanked by two of the women teachers, Mrs Farndell (left) and Mrs Wellings. The Lewises' daughter, Ruth, is seated sixth from the left on the far side of the long table. Bob Butchers, who provided the photograph, sits two places down from Ruth. Note the runner for the sliding partition doors on the floor to the left.

The School History That Never Was

This account of a 1959 school reunion, now to be found in the library of the Sussex Archaeological Society, is all that survives of a LOGS history planned by Cecil Lewis.

It includes the occasional typing error, but in view of his cavalier way with the records (*see page 94*), we can count it a miracle that even this faint glimpse of the school in days long gone has come down to us.

The numbers taking part in a mass football match in the 1920s are a testimony to the success of the school in Canon Griffiths' time, and perhaps we shouldn't be surprised to learn that even that worthy cleric was prepared to wield the cane to keep order.

Major Legge, apart from his interest in ornithology, was also something of an expert on postage stamps. A Google search shows him to have been the author of *Commonwealth of Australia – The Line Engraved Issues of 1914, and the Essays, Die and Plate Proofs of the Georgian 1d* and *The 1913 Penny Kangaroo of Australia.*

LEWES OLD GRAMMAR SCHOOL REUNION   SUNDAY 13 DECEMBER 1959

In connection with the proposed publication of a history of Lewes Old Grammar School, a reunion of Old Boys was held at the School on Sunday 13 December.

Owing to the inclement weather, only a handful of the oldest Old Boys who had accepted the invitation were able to come, but as it happened these four stalwarts, led by the oldest, Mr Arthur Broadbent of Lewes, who was at the School in 1893, covered between them a period of nearly 40 years in the history of the school, thus providing in their fascinating reminiscences a continuing narrative, each one carrying on the story from his predecessor.

Mr Broadbent recalled that in 1885 his brilliant oldest brother, Theodore Parker Broadbent, who had also been a pupil at the school, had obtained the Scholarship that had just been founded in honour of Thomas Hughes, author of 'Tom Brown's Schooldays' at Oriel College, Oxford, and became a Unitarian minister at Cheltenham before his tragically early death at the age of 26. Mr Broadbent still treasures a postcard written to him by his brother in Latin in 1890. enclosing money for him to buy fireworks with on Bonfire night. Mr Broadbent recalled that in one Summer term he took 75 (or perhaps it was 85?) wickets for an average of 3.75 runs.

Mr T Reader White,(Mayor of Lewes in 1889) retired from The Headmastership in in 1893 and was succeeded by the Rev. Henry Cruikshank, who temporarily changed the name of the school to 'St Kenelm's College (having been warden of St Kenelm's School, Brighton, before coming to Lewes).

The second speaker was Mr R P Cheale who left the School in 1897 and until this reunion had never since set foot in the building. He recalled that Mr Pearce, an assistant under T R White, had seceded from the School and set up on his own at Barton House, on the site of the present Town Hall Offices in Fisher Street. During the Headmastership of the Rev Dr E E Hodgson (1896 - 1905) a School Chapel was built, and a ship's bell used to summon the boys to Service. Later on the Chapel was converted into a chemistry laboratory. Strict discipline prevailed in those days but, Mr Cheale said 'we were very fond of our masters, and his school days were 'some of the happiest of my life'.

Major H D Legge of Pulborough. son of the late Dr W Heneage Legge of Ringmer, who left the School in 1911, took up the tale and declared that as pupil, head boy and subsequently pupil teacher, he owed a great deal to the school. At that time, during the headmastership of Mr Shepherd Smith, there were 40 boarders, but Major Legge himself often walked to school, learning his history, divinity and Shakespeare as he came over the Downs from Ringmer and collecting over a hundred varieties of birds' eggs on the way. He recalled football matches   between day boys and boarders,and 'nightshirts v. pyjamas' as well as between Oxford and Cambridge supporters, played with a tennis ball on BoatRace Day. Major Legge himself founded a school Bonfire Society and as Headboy in 1909, he wrote and delivered a Latin letter to the Judge before the opening of the Assizes, requesting the traditional half holiday for the School. (It is, however, still not clear when this custom began.)

The fourth and final speaker, Mr Hughes, who was at the school from 1921 to 1929, in the time of the late Canon Griffiths, and whose son is now at the school, told of the memorable visit to Snowdon which Canon Griffiths organised on the occasion of the total eclipse of the sun in 1927. To ensure discipline on on the long journey the headmaster took his cane with him and, Mr Hughes recalled, had to use it on one or two recalcitrants from Newhaven but otherwise even though rain obscured the eclipse itself. Mr Hughes also recalled 'Oxford versus Cambridge' football matches in the 1920s when 170 players participated, all struggling with one ball. All in all, Mr Hughes concluded, it was the 'grandest time of my life'.

It may be of interest to record that the oldest surviving old boy of the school, Mr Henry J Barratt of The Avenue, Lewes, who will be 90 in February and who was unfortunately only able to be with us in spirit came to the school in 1883 having already been a pupil under T Reader White at Cliffe House Academy before that establishment closed and Mr White transferred to the Grammar School which had been the Anglican rival of the Non-conformist Cliffe Academy throughout the nineteenth century.

'I didn't like him, I have to say. He'd walk right past you in the street, even after you'd left the school – an odd character. He would regularly set us work and disappear for a lot of the lesson.

'There was just a handful of boarders then, but most of us were day boys and girls, and we went home for lunch.

'Our football pitch was up on the Downs, in the valley to the left of the road leading up to the racecourse. It was known as "the motor road", because motor trials were held there – the cars would go up one of two parallel roads and come back down the other. Our football shirts were maroon-and-white quarters. One season the Brighton and Hove Albion player Len Darling coached us, illustrating tactics on a blackboard in the classroom.

'Cricket and athletics were held at the Phoenix ground (owned by the ironworks), which we reached through the back entrance to the school in Paddock Road. The adjacent field was Baxter's, belonging to the printers at the top of School Hill.'

Jackie Battams (then Woodhams) joined the school in 1942 at the age of five and found Lewis 'rather frightening for a young girl. He seemed extremely large to me, and he always walked around in his gown. His wife was a motherly person, though.

'All the classes were held in one large room on the right of the front door. It went the whole length of the building and was lit by a stove. There was a wooden hut outside for the senior classes. We'd walk right through the school to Baxter's Field for games.'

"The place was never redecorated. In my last term I wrote my name and the date on the ceiling of the end dormitory. Fifteen years later I was making a delivery to the school and took the opportunity of looking around. My inscription was still there."

"There was a lot of bullying, and the boys could make the lives of weak masters a misery. One of them was sacked, and Mr Lewis almost encouraged us to persecute him. He rode a motorbike, and on his last day some of the boys put sugar in the tank. I can still see him wheeling his Beezer Bantam towards the Bottleneck with a jeering crowd in pursuit."

Rev Lewis and the school choir outside St Anne's church c. 1956. The school held its Festival of Nine Lessons and Carols at the church every Christmas. The church organist stands on the right.

1952–
Reign of Elizabeth II

MISTAKEN IDENTITY

The twinning of Lewes with Waldshut-Tiengen followed Robert Seiz's employment as a German assistant during the 1957–1958 academic year.

Young Seiz wasn't the first or last person to confuse the town's two grammar schools. He arrived at the invitation of the state school in Mountfield Road, but was wrongly directed to LOGS instead.

Cecil Lewis took pity on the confused teacher and put him up at the school for a short period while he sorted himself out. The rest is twinning history.

Badge commemorating LGB Brass of Lewes performing at Waldshut.

Ann Baker arrived in January 1944, also aged five, and by July 1951 she was one of only two girls remaining.

'Rev Lewis was rather gruff, but I quite liked him. If he wanted to go down the town for a drink he'd give you a maths test and leave you to it. His wife was one of the teachers, and she could be strict. She'd give you a rap over the knuckles if you misbehaved. Once when a friend blew on his macaroni and accidentally got it on his clothes she gave all three of us a thousand lines. A thousand! I was an obedient girl, and I did them.

'The kindergarten was on the ground floor. You went through it to class 2, and then classes 3 and 4 were in the big room with a partittition. The fifth form worked in a prefabricated building outside. The boys and girls learned together, but sat separately. It was all extremely old-fashioned.

'I learned to read before I went to school, and I helped some of the others with their reading. At the time I should have gone up to the next class I was kept down, and when my mother enquired about it she was told that it was because I was useful. She said "I don't pay for her to be useful," and Mr Lewis agreed.

'There were about twenty children in the kindergarten then, and twenty-four in the other classes. We got our maroon blazers from Cootes, the outfitters on School Hill. We had a good level of 11-plus passes, and most children left at that age.'

For Tony Elphick, who would later take over the family's garden shop in the Cliffe, Lewis was 'a strange cove'. He was a pupil during the war, and recalls everyone going down into the cellar to sit on piles of coke when the air raid siren sounded.

'The school wasn't a kind place,' he says. 'There was a lot of bullying, and the classes were huge – up to forty children. We had a Miss Cole in the kindergarten who was brilliant, but after that I didn't enjoy it at all. It was a kind of place that wouldn't survive today, and I was glad to move on to secondary school.'

Derek Swain was one of those who *didn't* leave at eleven. A farmer's son, he came to the school in early 1945, just before his eighth birthday, and he boarded until he left in July 1952.

'There were about two dozen boarders then,' he recalls. 'Most stayed there only during the week, but a few of us were termly boarders.

'The food was appalling, and there was very little of it. It was just like Oliver Twist. I'd get so hungry that I would cadge food from the day pupils, and in the evening after prep I'd go to the kitchen and swipe lumps of bread from the old clay bin.

'For breakfast they gave you a little bit of porridge – about three mouthfuls – and perhaps an equally small amount of scrambled egg. I'd literally lick my plate clean. The tea came in a big old urn with a tap, and it was like dishwater.

'I once took a piece of chocolate from a master's drawer and was found out. Of course I got the cane for that: into the dining room and bend over. The cane left you with black-and-blue marks.

'Lewis had lost his first wife – a lovely lady – and married one of the teachers, Miss Baker. She was always smiling. They had a young daughter who was amazingly intelligent.

'I remember Lewis as short and thickset with a round, blotchy, red face and glasses. He always wore his black gown. He wasn't easy to like, and his staff didn't stay long. He did have feelings, though. When the time came for me to leave I went to shake his hand and he was very emotional. I said "Goodbye, sir," and he started crying.'

Cecil Lewis playing the organ at Southover church.

School sports day at the Paddock.

A DAUGHTER REMEMBERS

*Ann Lewis (now Milland) had a unique insider's view of LOGS as a child.
Her father was the headmaster, her mother was the geography teacher
and the school building was her home from the age of four.*

" I was born in 1948, when my parents
lived at Ringles Cross, Uckfield (my father
would drive his black MG to school every
morning), but a few years later we moved
into the school.

An early memory is playing with the
wonderful Mr Reed, who was the cleaner
and odd job man for all the years we were
there. He lived on the Landport estate and
had thirteen children. One night I wrote on
one of the blackboards 'Silly old headmaster'.
The next day I went off to school and came
home to find that the boys had got into big
trouble, everyone thinking it was them.

My father wasn't backward in giving a
boy a good caning. He would stand them on
the upstairs landing, where they would take
the consequences for whatever they had
done: none seemed any the worse for it.

I suppose you could say that he didn't
suffer fools gladly, and he was certainly of
the old school. I well remember the classes
chanting their times tables every morning
and, my goodness, they knew them!

I know that he could be very awkward
and rude at times, but he did have quite a
sense of humour and to me he was a great
father. I should add that he did have his
problems. He and my mother lost twin boys
before I was born, and a solicitor who was
also a mayor of Lewes embezzled his money
(probably from the sale of the Uckfield
house) and was jailed for it.

*Cecil and Nancy Lewis, née Baker. They married
in 1945.*

Sometimes it was hard growing up in a mainly boys school. I used to get whistled at, which is not something you want at the age of eight or nine. When I got to about 15 or 16 I had my first boyfriend. He used to walk me home from my school, and one day I got severely told off because we were having a bit of a kiss between the front door and the glass door just behind it, and some of the boys saw us and thought it was great fun.

My bedroom was in what is now one of the classrooms – upstairs on the left when you look at the school from the road. The cook was Lucy Wilson, who lived in the room at the bottom of the stairs on the first floor and was like a second mother to me.

There was definitely a funny feeling at that end of the house, and after my father closed the boarders' department those rooms remained empty for many years. I would never go along that back passage by myself. Lucy said she had seen a grey lady walking up there, and I used to wonder if it was perhaps the first Mrs Lewis! Lucy later moved into the attic on the third floor, and we both had a nasty feeling up there, too. I discovered years later that one of the boarders had hanged himself there. **"**

Ann with the school caretaker, Fred Reed.

Cecil Lewes (left) and the young Ann with a group of LOGS boarders on the beach at Newhaven.

"Mr Lewis was very keen on Latin. One day he asked me why the sports trophy was called the Victor Ludorum cup. I thought on my feet and said I supposed it had been donated by someone of that name. I got a whack around the head and a hundred lines."

"Careers advice was almost non-existent. The school advertisements boasted about success in the Royal Navy exams, and I thought that was a good idea, but the careers officer said he'd put me down for the Civil Service. I protested that I liked boats, so he compromised by specifying Customs & Excise."

Opposite page: Mike Parker's 1959 report, marking the last attempt to teach Latin at LOGS.

Right: Cecil Lewis's school in 1960. The headmaster sits in the middle of his staff, wearing glasses.

When Philip Murphy came to LOGS in 1953 all the girls and the boarders had gone, and the Lewis family were living upstairs.

'Lewis taught us Latin and Religious Knowledge,' he says. 'I thought he was the worst kind of schoolmaster. Although I have heard good things said about him, I found him unapproachable, cold and irritable. I do remember a lad putting one on him when he was threatened with the cane.

'Most of the pupils at that time were offspring of the Lewes "great and good" – dentists, doctors, surveyors and so on. They regarded it as a respectable school where their sons and daughters didn't have to mix with the rougher elements. They thought they were doing their best for their children, but it wasn't a place which encouraged much brain-power.'

By the time Mike Parker arrived in 1957, Latin had been dropped, and he experienced a fleeting attempt to reintroduce it. That failed after a term, so at last ending the classics teaching which had been the staple of Agnes Morley's medieval school.

'Lewis had some strange ways. The homework he gave us would very often be exactly the same as we'd had only a few days earlier, so I'd just copy it out again. He never noticed. No wonder I never did well at English.

'The whistle blew at the end of every break, and we had to form lines for a finger-nail inspection – and then wash our hands if they weren't up to standard. There was a strict uniform code, and you had to stand whenever a teacher or a visitor came into the classroom.

'At times Lewis could be jovial, but he was often in a bad mood. He would come into the classroom during another teacher's lesson and bark out, "Are you paying attention, boy?" Of course you were, but he'd grab the short hair at the back of your neck, which was excruciating, and bang your forehead on the desk.

'I quite enjoyed the food, especially the puddings. We had a two-course lunch, with the older pupils serving the younger ones at table.

1953
Commonwealth team climbs Everest; Queen's coronation

1954
Rationing ends

1956
Suez Crisis

1957
Harold Macmillan becomes Conservative prime minister

1960
Macmillan makes 'Wind of Change' speech; floods in Lewes

Flooding by the Grange, 1960

1961
Berlin Wall built; University of Sussex founded

1962
Cuban Missile Crisis

1963
President Kennedy assassinated; Beeching Report begins UK rail closures

'We queued once a week to pay our dinner money. Lewis would be seated behind the table, and when he called out 'seven and six' or whatever it was, you threw the coins into a chalk box in front of him. He couldn't check it, so I would always keep the odd sixpence back, and I'm sure most of the other boys did, too.

'Art was taught in the first-floor room to the left of the main entrance. It was completely unfurnished up there, with ricketty stairs and passageways, and no carpets.

'The one really good teacher was Mr Morgan, who took us for maths, sport and music. On our last day, in 1962, he invited us down to the Volunteer pub at the bottom of town and treated everyone to a light ale.'

A NEW BROOM

It was in 1962 that Roy Mead travelled down from London to be interviewed for a teaching post at Lewes Old Grammar School. His account of the experience highlights the eccentricities of the man who (against all the odds) was to become his headmaster.

'I motored down from Ilford, and it wasn't such an easy journey in those days. The front of the building was as it is now. There was a steep playground behind and an old green hut.

Fried Lettuce à la LOGS

Lunchtimes during the early Sixties were a frugal affair for the children and the staff, but certainly not for the headmaster himself. While everyone else made do with little more than soup and an apple, Roy Mead recalls, Cecil Lewis tucked into a three-course meal.

On one occasion the parents were asked to make a contribution to refreshments at a forthcoming sports day, and Lewis posted a notice on the board detailing how much each had given.

When the day arrived it emerged that all the children were to get for their parents' generosity was a serving of lettuce sandwiches.

As it happened, the weather turned bad and sports day had to be cancelled. What a treat awaited everyone the following lunchtime: fried lettuce sandwiches!

'I sat waiting for half an hour, and then a head came round the door. It said abruptly, "I don't think you're the right man for the job," and disappeared. After another interval a woman came in and asked if anyone had been to see me. I told her what had happened, and she explained that that was her husband, the headmaster, and that, thank you very much, I obviously hadn't got the job.

'Some days later I had another letter from the school asking me for an interview, so I drove all the way down again – and exactly the same thing happened. It was like something out of a Dickens novel. In fact I soon found that the school in those days was very similar to Dotheboys Hall.

'I now applied for other jobs, and I found one in Worthing. I had actually signed a contract with them when I received a letter from Cecil Lewis which said, "You will start work on such-and-such a date, and you will be paid such-and-such a year, six monthly in arrears."

'I'm a Christian, so I prayed about this, and the upshot was that, despite everything, I excused myself from the Worthing post and joined the staff of LOGS.'

The school of which he had become a part was by now a very small one, and his senior class consisted of only four boys. One of them was John Copper, a member of the famous folk singing family from Rottingdean – and he paints a memorable picture of an institution which had been preserved in Victorian aspic.

'I went there in 1959, at the age of 12,' he remembers, 'and by the time I left it was down to about forty pupils between the ages of four and seventeen. There was the kindergarten with a few girls in it, and then forms 2, 3a and 3b (they shared the hall) and 5, in the shed outside.

'It was a very strange school – formal, quirkily individual and from another age. We had a matron and a cook, for instance, and that's what we always had to call them. When I told my dad, Bob, about the things that happened he urged me never to forget them. He was a great collector of old songs, and would later write about the old ways himself. "Take note of all this," he would say to me, "because it's disappeared everywhere else. Anyone can be modern, but you're in touch with something genuinely ancient."

Cecil Lewis without his dog collar.

One of the Copper Family's compilations. John Copper was at the school from 1959 until 1964 and loved its antique flavour.

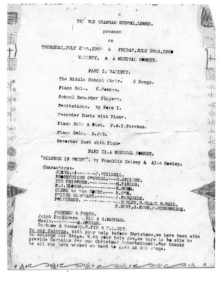

'Cecil Lewis must already have been in his seventies when I went there. I found him a lovely, dear old soul, homely and completely old-fashioned. Think of W.C. Fields and you've got the idea. He was a little overweight, and he would come puffing into assembly in the morning, often with one of his trouser legs caught in his long johns. He was a bit of a musician, although he played the piano pretty badly, and we had a choir which once performed at the Dome in Brighton.

'I got off to a good start with his wife, who taught us geography, because dad had made a study of some of the local field layouts where we lived, with their names and so on, and I brought in a map which quite excited her.

'The discipline was strict, and you didn't disobey. I remember one afternoon, when I was about thirteen, Lewis told me to stand under the clock upstairs – a routine punishment – and he forgot all about me. The hours passed, the school bell rang for the end of the day, and I didn't dare move. Eventually he found me and told me he'd better run me to the station in his grey Rover 90.

'Of course, from an academic point of view it was pretty ropey. I came out with a love of Shakespeare, but there were whole areas of the curriculum we never covered. Nobody could possibly have taken an 'A' level there. I wanted to be an engineer, and when I went for an interview at the technical college they told me I'd need 'O' level physics to get in. Physics? We'd never even touched the subject! I had to do a crash course to get in.

'You could sense the change of atmosphere when Roy Mead arrived. The two of them didn't get on at all – chalk and cheese. Mead wanted to change things, and Lewis was still in that other world.'

UNDER NEW MANAGEMENT

One day in 1964, as Roy Mead tells it, 'Lewis banged me in the ribs, took me into the dining room and said, "Do you want to buy the school?" He seemed to want an immediate answer, because when I told him I needed to talk to my wife about it he asked me who wore the trousers in our family.'

He was, indeed, interested, but there was a problem. Lewis offered him a private mortgage to buy the school for £10,000, but

---

VICIOUS CYCLE

Cecil Lewis enjoyed outdoor pursuits, and to celebrate his 80th birthday (a year before he left the school) he walked over the Downs to Brighton in a snowstorm with his two Jack Russell terriers, Robert and Jill.

He was a keen cyclist, but disliked pedalling uphill. On sports days at the Convent Field he would ride his bike down Rotten Row at a great lick.

'He had no brakes,' Roy Mead later recalled, 'and so he would simply shout "Get out of the way!" as he careered down the slope.'

Once the games were over he handed the bike to Mead and instructed him to wheel it back up the hill to school.

Facing page: LOGS drama. Above left, 'The Pirates of Penzance' c. 1958; below (and playbill) 'Silence in Court', July 1960.

1964

*Labour government under
Harold Wilson; Mods & Rockers
fight on Brighton seafront*

1965

US send troops to Vietnam

1966

*Aberfan disaster, landslip
killing 116 children and
28 adults; England win
football world cup*

1968

*Martin Luther King and
Robert Kennedy assassinated*

he wanted a deposit of £2,000, and when Mead approached his friendly local bank manager in Worthing he found his request for a loan refused point-blank. The manager had taken the precaution of contacting his Lewes branch, and local intelligence about the school was damning: 'Don't touch it with a bargepole'.

The money had to be borrowed in dribs and drabs from his family ('£30 here, £50 there') until the full sum had been raised.

'Lewis, typically for him, said there was no need for any paperwork and that a gentlemen's agreement should suffice, but I of course insisted that everything was made legally binding.

'We signed the contract on the eve of the general election in October 1964. Harold Wilson's Labour government came in and immediately announced that it was going to get rid of all the independent schools at a stroke!'

UP IN FLAMES

There was time for one final, inexplicable act by the retiring headmaster. Quite how much material he had accumulated it is impossible to say, but before relinquishing the building to his successor, Cecil Lewis carried the school records into the yard – and burned the lot.

The Mead Years

I T WASN'T REALLY A GRAMMAR SCHOOL in those days, Roy Mead would later say, but a prep school for children from five years upwards. That was something he was determined to change. The LOGS story during his decades at the helm was to be one of a gradual but profound transformation – a broadening of the intake (a sixth form, a full complement of girls); an expansion of premises (the King Henry's Road site, St Clair and Tyne houses); a change in status (to a charitable trust); and the restoration of its academic reputation.

The 1851 building would later be re-named Mead House in honour of its long-serving owner, headmaster and trustee.

He officially took over from Cecil Lewis in May 1965, and began by taking a bold step which showed his intent: the fees were immediately doubled to £40 a term. Having worked alongside the staff for some time, he knew which ones he wanted to keep and which to weed out. At his inaugural assembly there were only 35 pupils, but a photograph of the school during his first full year (*below*) shows that the numbers quickly increased. Within two years he had a hundred on the books, and his ten-year mortgage on the building was paid off in five.

Roy Mead (centre, two rows behind young girl) with staff and pupils in 1965–1966, his first full year in charge.

1969
Voting age reduced from 21 to 18; capital punishment abolished; Priory School formed from amalgamation of the Lewes boys' and girls' grammar schools with the secondary modern

In the end, the Labour government's intention of integrating the nation's private schools into the state system came to nothing. What *did* disappear in many parts of England and Wales were the grammar schools. The creation of comprehensives from the late 1960s was (and remains) controversial, and it gave a boost to those private schools which could show that they provided a quality alternative to what the state had to offer.

'In a way Cecil Lewis had been his own worst enemy,' Mead judged. 'He was a very good teacher, and because he got nearly all of his pupils through their exams, they moved on once they reached the age of eleven. I was looking to turn LOGS into a proper grammar school with a junior department, so that we were catering for five- to 18-year-olds.'

NEW GROWTH

In 1968, with the building already bursting at the seams, new premises became available for rent a few doors along the street. The fine old house at no. 141 was owned by a Dr Tack, who lived in Canada. One of its previous uses had been as a private club, but at this time it housed the Inland Revenue, which was about to move to Medwyn House in Mountfield Road.

LOGS rented no. 141 High Street in 1968 and bought it three years later. Eventually named St Clair House, it was at first home to the school's junior department.

Mead quickly did a deal which gave him first option to buy the property for £14,000 should Tack decide to sell. That became a reality in 1971, and a local building society now felt sufficiently confident in the school to grant him a 100 per cent mortgage.

Space had also become a problem for the fast expanding sixth form. Once again the solution was to find rented accommodation, in this case involving the staff in a few minutes' walk along the high street. Two floors were rented above the Nationwide Building Society, and the sixth formers would remain there until the purchase of Tyne House in 1994.

Roy Mead never doubted the wisdom of his decision to cater for the older age group, but the abrasive side of his nature was provoked by a visit from a schools' inspector.

'It seemed to me that he was more interested in the flooring than in the academic standards,' he recalled later. 'He told me that I'd never succeed. The whole country was going in for sixth form colleges, and I'd be much better off forgetting about it and concentrating on the younger pupils.

'Well, that was a red rag to a bull as far as I was concerned, and our numbers quickly grew.'

St Clair House had previously housed the Lewes and County Club, and today's DT room behind it was originally built as a squash court – reputedly one of the first in England.

The expanding Sixth Form occupied rooms above the Nationwide Building Society.

Under new management: Roy Mead and his wife Isabel, née St Clair. She was the school's head of science.

1970

Edward Heath is Tory prime minister

1971

Open University begins teaching; decimal currency introduced

1973

Britain joins Common Market

1974

Harold Wilson re-elected

1976

Wilson retires, and James Callaghan is prime minister

1979

'Winter of discontent', with widespread strikes; Margaret Thatcher becomes the UK's first woman prime minister; opening of the Cuilfail Tunnel in Lewes

HERE COME THE GIRLS

The most profound change of all, however, was the merging of LOGS with Lewes High School for Girls (formerly Leicester House School) in King Henry's Road. Mead's earlier dealings with it had been less than welcoming: keen to promote drama, he had asked whether the girls might like to join the boys in theatrical productions which included female roles, only to be rebuffed on the grounds that such mingling of the sexes was inappropriate – 'although many of them were sisters of our boys'.

Now, though, times were tough for the High School. First Mead was asked whether he would care to run it under the existing regime (he declined) and then he was invited to buy it outright. Having agreed in principle, he attended a parents' meeting late in 1976 and was given a hostile reception. His reputation as a fierce disciplinarian at LOGS had gone before him. ('Yes, I did use the cane occasionally for serious offences, but always after consultation with the parents.')

But Mead knew something that hadn't been revealed to the girls' families. He told the meeting that he would bow to their wishes and withdraw his offer, but they should realise that the school was bankrupt and wouldn't still be there at Christmas if nobody came forward to buy it.

'With that I stepped down from the stage and made to leave, whereupon they clamoured for me to come back. I assured them that I wasn't the ogre they imagined, and that the boys were happy at LOGS. Yes, some were naughty, but they were treated fairly, and the girls' school would be run properly.'

It was, when he bought it in January 1977, 'a shambles', with no fewer than 45 teachers (albeit some of them part-time) for 60 pupils, nine teaching English in the fifth year. He retained just four of them, including the headmistress, Miss Diamond.

DO-IT-YOURSELF

Although Mead believed that boys and girls should be taught separately, the constant toing and froing between St Anne's Hill and the Wallands area soon became wearing for staff who had to teach at both sites. The solution was obvious, and in 1979 the junior school and the senior girls switched homes.

The way it was done, on a single summer's day, was typical of the headmaster's approach. While the juniors were sent off to Drusilla's Zoo and a lorry transported the heaviest furniture, the remaining pupils and staff walked back and forth, hour after hour, ferrying equipment from one building to the other.

'They had a wonderful time,' was Mead's verdict. 'You could do that in those days. It makes me so cross that you can't get them to do anything now.

'We used to get them in to help paint and decorate, too. They wouldn't let anyone spoil the work they'd done.'

> ### TEN THOUSAND UNMENTIONABLES
>
> When Roy Mead took over the girls' school he found twenty rented television sets stored in cupboards, unused. To the rental company's claim that the school was under contract, he replied briskly that the sets would be lined up on the pavement outside for collection. They were duly reclaimed.
>
> He was flummoxed, however, by another legacy for which no suitable home could be found – a job lot of ten thousand pairs of grey knickers.

The girls' school in King Henry's Road soon became the home of the LOGS junior department, Morley House.

1980

Iranian Embassy siege in London

1982

Falklands War

1984

Miners' strike; IRA bomb Grand Hotel, Brighton

1987

'Hurricane' ravages southern England

1988

Lockerbie air crash

In similar fashion, Mead had a new block put up on the western flank of the main school without employing a building firm. He found two local builders and supervised their work himself. When a lorry delivered 10,000 bricks at eight o'clock one morning the second-year boys were on hand to pass them hand-over-hand down the alleyway for forty minutes. Job done!

As for the building behind the school hall, Mead got his brother to put up the lavatories, changing room and the classroom above with the aid of volunteer sixth formers.

The girl brickies

Not long after taking over the girls' school, Roy Mead ordered a large quantity of bricks to be delivered for an extension, and (in his usual way) asked the girls to bring old clothes and gloves to school the next morning so that they could help carry them in.

His home telephone was busy all evening, with alarmed parents protesting, some claiming that their daughters' child-bearing prospects in later life would be endangered by what they saw as heavy labour.

Mead invited them to the main school at 9 o'clock the next morning, but found an angry posse waiting for him half an hour earlier than that.

'They told me that I didn't understand girls, although I had two daughters of my own. We had a long discussion in my room, during which I kept an eye on the clock.

'At a quarter past nine I told them that perhaps they were right, and I put a call through to the girls' school. "Put me through to Miss Diamond," I said – and then, "Miss Diamond, will you please tell the girls that they're not to move the bricks after all."

'Miss Diamond apologised. "I'm terribly sorry," she told me, "but it's already been done."

'All I could do was offer to take the names of all the girls, and to ask the parents to let me know if they had any gynaecological problems when they reached their twenties and got married.'

THE PLAY'S THE THING

It was, of course, Roy Mead who had the stage built at the rear of the school hall. He was, after all, something of a showman. In his early days in Lewes as a master under Cecil Lewis he had entertained the children with his magic shows, and after he took over the school he produced plays and comic operas year after year, occasionally (*see below*) more than one at a time.

The idea was to involve as many of the pupils as possible, and their performances ranged from Agatha Christie who-dunnits to excerpts from Shakespeare. The 1984 play was 'Jennings Abounding' by Anthony Buckeridge, who had a special reason for being in the audience: not only did he and his wife Eileen live nearby in Barcombe, but she was on the staff of LOGS as head of English.

Programme cover for the LOGS 1983 drama festival, and the producer's notes in which Roy Mead describes the idea of performing two plays in one week as 'completely mad'.

THE
OLD GRAMMAR SCHOOL
LEWES

*Drama Festival
1983*

PRESENTING

TEN LITTLE INDIANS

By AGATHA CHRISTIE

RELATIVELY SPEAKING

By ALAN AYCKBOURN

SOUVENIR PROGRAMME   30p

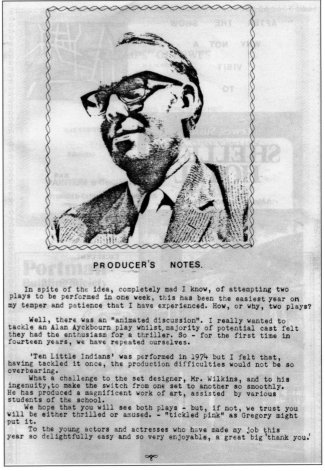

PRODUCER'S NOTES.

In spite of the idea, completely mad I know, of attempting two plays to be performed in one week, this has been the easiest year on my temper and patience that I have experienced. How, or why, two plays?

Well, there was an "animated discussion". I really wanted to tackle an Alan Ayckbourn play whilst, majority of potential cast felt they had the enthusiasm for a thriller. So - for the first time in fourteen years, we have repeated ourselves.

'Ten Little Indians' was performed in 1974 but I felt that, having tackled it once, the production difficulties would not be so overbearing.

What a challenge to the set designer, Mr. Wilkins, and to his ingenuity, to make the switch from one set to another so smoothly. He has produced a magnificent work of art, assisted by various students of the school.

We hope that you will see both plays - but, if not, we trust you will be either thrilled or amused. - "tickled pink" as Gregory might put it.

To the young actors and actresses who have made my job this year so delightfully easy and so very enjoyable, a great big 'thank you.'

THIS SPORTING LIFE

It may be small in numbers, but LOGS has always shown a brave willingness to compete in sporting events against much larger schools . . .

When Ian Turner was a keen all-round athlete at LOGS from 1968–1972 he once suffered the indignity of being sent home by Roy Mead at a school sport's day for refusing to tuck his shirt into his shorts.

'Roy was a stickler for etiquette,' he recalls, 'and when we competed against other local schools he was often very put out by their slovenly attitudes. We always had to turn out in immaculate cricket whites, for instance, and we always had to be on our best behaviour.

'But my love of cricket came from him. He made sport a vital part of school life, and was a cricket umpire himself.'

After living abroad, and playing semi-professional football in Zimbabwe, Ian returned to teach sport at LOGS under Roy Mead in 1983, working his way up to head of department before leaving in 2006. He was chairman of the Lewes and District Primary Schools Sports Association, and organised the first ever Sussex Schools Under-11 girls' cricket, which involved many LOGS pupils.

'What gave me most pleasure during my time there,' he says, 'was extending those contacts with other schools, and so helping integrate LOGS into the Lewes way of life.

'Of course we often had to put out teams from a mixed age-range because of our size, but we took part in a wide range of sports – running, swimming, cricket, football and rugby – and we were very successful.'

Teacher tips talented twosome to go far

LEWES Old Grammar School overcame the odds to reach the final of the Sussex Schools U19 Cup by beating a succession of much bigger comprehensives. The final, against The Weald School in Horsham, takes place on February 5.

Coach Iain Turner (back row, far right) said: 'It's a great achievement for such a small school. We've only got about 30 lads to pick from in the whole sixth form.'

Iain also believes that two of his players, 17-year old Steve King and 18-year old Jack Ogden, are easily good enough to play County League football.

'They're the two best prospects I've seen in 20-odd years, with the possible exception of the Johnson twins. Steve's at Eastbourne United and is definitely good enough for the first team, and think both lads will play for Sussex next year.'

Ian Turner with his successful under-19 football team in 2001.

A fellow athlete during Ian's time as a pupil at LOGS was Nick Akers, a successful middle-distance runner who won his biggest headlines a few years later by becoming the first sportsman to change his name to attract sponsorship.

'Mick Gale was my PE teacher and running coach at LOGS,' Nick remembers, 'and he moved to New Zealand to teach. When I finished my A-levels in 1974 I'd left it too late to apply for university, so when he asked me if I wanted to join him out there in order to run, I packed my bags and went.'

His performances won him a place on the Cayman Islands' team at the 1978 Commonwealth Games, and this prompted him to set his sights on entering the Moscow Olympics two years later. But how could he afford to take part?

Direct sponsorship was impossible in those amateur times, but the makers of Vladivar Vodka in Warrington saw an opportunity. They would make a donation to the Cayman Islands Olympics team if he would change his name to Nick Vladivar.

'They flew me to Manchester from Canada, where I was now living. We did the press and photo ops, and £10,000 was pledged to the Cayman athletes.'

Unfortunately, politics intervened. A US-inspired boycott of the Games because of the Soviet Union's war in Afghanistan meant that Nick never fulfilled his Olympic dream – and he ruefully changed his name back to plain Nick Akers.

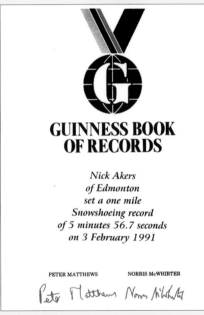

GUINNESS BOOK OF RECORDS

*Nick Akers
of Edmonton
set a one mile
Snowshoeing record
of 5 minutes 56.7 seconds
on 3 February 1991*

PETER MATTHEWS   NORRIS McWHIRTER

JON'S SPORTING TYPES

'In lane one, Nick Vladivar, two Johnny Walker, three Mick Martini, Sid Schweppes, Don Dubonnet . . .'

*Left: Nick Akers in his LOGS years with a collection of trophies.
Right: In Canada Nick took up snow-shoeing – with great success.*

A Daily Mail cartoonist's take on Nick's name change.

ROD OF IRON

The regime under Roy Mead was undeniably severe, and many former pupils, teachers and parents recall being afraid to cross him and stir his anger.

'He was an excellent headmaster in that he cared for the children above everything else,' says Diana Hope, who had a son and two daughters at LOGS and also worked for twenty years as secretary of the junior school. 'Our three all went to university and became PhDs, which speaks for itself. And if they had a problem he would always take the trouble to listen and to deal with it. He was super in those circumstances.

'But he regarded the parents as a burden he had to put up with, and he could be very fierce with them. He sent out frequent newsletters, and he instructed us to keep them, making it very clear that he didn't want to have the office bothered with queries about matters he had already dealt with. I religiously did as I was told and so I still have the full set of those newsletters from 1978 right through to 2004. Well, he didn't say how long we had to keep them!

'When I first worked as secretary I queried why I hadn't been paid and was told that I was a volunteer and could only have petrol money. Eventually I *was* paid, a little. Mr Mead used to take the cost of the tea and coffee from our wages before we got them, and when I explained that I only worked mornings and shouldn't have the full amount deducted he was furious. What really annoyed him was that I had dared to talk about such things with other members of staff. He hated discussions about money.

'The junior school once used Tesco tokens to buy a computer, and they hadn't consulted him first. He went wild. I thought he was going to blow a fuse. Fortunately Eileen Buckeridge was on hand to calm things down – she was lovely.'

Diana's husband John served on the PTA, and remembers some tempestuous meetings.

'Everything was fine if we agreed with him, and he'd take our ideas on board if they suited him, but otherwise he didn't really want to listen. On one occasion he became so angry with us that he got up and stormed out.'

"He told us that if our daughters were 'stupid enough' to have their ears pierced they could only wear studs, and that if a boy came to school with his hair too long he would be taken to have it cut – and his parents would be sent the bill."

'A barber used to come into the school during my time there. When I refused to have my hair cut short Mr Mead expelled me, and that was the end of my time at LOGS. Ironically enough, I'm bald now."

"My mother complained because I was given ten maths questions for homework. His response was to increase it to twenty."

I wish to cover in my letter some of the points I raised but first of all can I write a little about Angels and Saints. The maintenance of the high standard of discipline that we expect from the pupils at this school is difficult enough to achieve, with falling standards, lack of consideration and Angels and Saints. The angels in the "Dreadful Affair on the Midnight Express" are your children - and from what I am led to believe you must be saints to be able to look at the angels and then write to me in the firm belief that "he/she never done it, Mr.Mead. They wouldn't ever do such a thing." Every year I have to read the riot act about all manner of things. Then you find that youngsters of over eleven do not know how to use a toilet - in fact some adults are in this category too - That they don't know how to treat other people's property - that they don't even realise when they are not coming up to standard - that they don't use the words "please" and "thank you" at home. - (I have heard and seen pupils behaving in the most abominable way to their parents) - what am I to do?

I did mention that I expect all children at school, hard heartedly, whether there are shortages of oil or strikes. We can carry on and wear extra clothing, jump up and run round Baxter's every hour if there is no heating in the school. Work will always continue. People living 2 miles from Lewes can't get in because of the rail strike!! Nonsense, I say, Walk it!

I am sorry to have to be so forthright but the molly coddling that goes on today is sickening. Certainly, as a child I would have been ashamed to have given way to difficulty. Difficulties are always there to be overcome.

At the A.G.M. on Friday, which was well attended, I made an appeal. Please leave my private telephone alone at weekends. It is terribly aggravating to be answering the phone on school matters on Sundays. When one hears the erring parent saying, "I don't mean to disturb you, Mr. Mead, but ......" I just about explode at the other end. I feel like saying, "Well, why bother to waste 2p in doing exactly that?" But I expect that would be like water off a duck's back. Now please, for the next few weeks my private number is definitely 'out of bounds'. Even after that please, please - Never on Sunday!!

It can usually wait till Monday anyway. It's usually some emergency like "Johnny's got a sore thumb, so can he be excused games tomorrow?!!!" etc.

Many matters worry me but there are one or two I should like to get off my chest right away. There have already been several requests for time off. You know the sort of thing "Impossible to fix air travel at another time" - "Essential to go at this time" - "Haven't been away since last time"!! etc. Now I do understand - and sympathise. Do realise that I don't think it at all practical to "set work" - Would you really work hard and well five or six hours a day whilst on a visit to Timbuctoo?? And that's what it means just to attempt to keep up. I have a job to do. I shall do that job to the best of my ability and if I am allowed to do so. Often this sort of thing cuts the ground right out from under our feet - so please understand when I write back to say "I do not approve!" But have a good holiday just the same!! One young man has been removed from the school because of my disapproval over such a similar matter. I was very wrong to oppose it and to express my disapproval! What is one to do? I still feel that discipline, self discipline, self denial, priorities, values, loyal ties, emotions and countless other important facets of life and training are at stake in this small area - so I'll just do my job and hope that I have your support and understanding. My you should sit at my end of the telephone some days!! You'd all soon realise exactly why I take an apparently heartless line from time to time.

Extracts from the regular newsletters Roy Mead sent to parents. He had a reputation for speaking his mind – and expecting to be obeyed – on any issue which affected the children.

NOT TO BE MISSED

Apart from putting on magic shows and staging plays, Roy Mead seemed to relish those occasions on which he called the whole school to order for serious breaches of discipline.

Many pupils recall these dramatic 'blow-ups' (as they were popularly known), during which his ear-splitting voice could be heard a considerable distance away.

On one occasion, after some misdemeanour in the canteen, all pupils who ate school meals were ordered to gather in the hall for a showpiece dressing down.

A teacher hailed one lad as he entered: 'But surely you don't take lunch here, do you?'

'No sir,' came the instant reply, 'but I wouldn't miss this for anything!'

Mystery Man 4: the LOGS ghost

In October 1983 Beryl Wilkins, a teacher in the junior department, wrote an article in *Sussex Life* about the school's very own ghost in what we now know as Mead House. We reproduce her report here, with thanks to Beryl and the magazine.

Phantom footsteps are a perpetual cause for speculation at the Old Grammar School, Lewes.

'I've heard them on many occasions,' said Mr Roy Mead, the headmaster. 'What they are is a mystery, but I'm certain that they belong to a friendly presence, so it's welcome to stay here!'

Apparently, the pattern never varies. 'The front door is heard to open and close, followed by the sound of footsteps walking up the main stairs,' explained Mr Mead.

'They continue along the first floor corridor and up a second stairway. The strange thing is that there is a door at the bottom of the second flight of stairs, but the steps don't pause there, nor are there any sounds suggestive of a door being opened and closed.'

This door was hung less than ten years ago.

'The steps go along the corridor of the top storey and stop in the room at the end.'

A former member of the administration staff was sitting with friends in Shelley's Hotel, next to the Old Grammar School, when Mr Chris Lloyd, one of the teaching staff, came in 'looking like a ghost himself'.

That evening he had been in the school office, on the first floor, using the telephone, when he heard the front door open and close, followed by footsteps coming upstairs.

Knowing himself to be alone in the building, he investigated. There was nothing to be seen on the lighted stairs – but the sound of the steps drew nearer. They went directly past him, aong the corridor and up a second flight of stairs. At that point he cut short his telephone conversation and made a hasty departure.

'An eerie experience but, in retrospect, an effective way of getting a free brandy,' laughed Mr Lloyd.

Evidently there is a spine-chilling charm in the experience, for most witnesses give a similarly light-hearted account.

'I knew nothing about the footsteps until I heard them one night,' said another member of staff. 'It must have been about 11 o'clock – a reminder that it was time I went home.'

David Blackwell, who has taught at the school for many years, said, 'It must be 15 years ago that I heard them. I think it's a boozy sort of ghost – it doesn't show up until around closing time.'

Some intrepid senior boys are eager to stage a ghost hunt. However, their chances of success may be minimal, since group hauntings have so far proved to be against its working habit.

In 1512 the Free Grammar School, as the Old Grammar School was originally called, was founded – mainly through the bequest of Agnes Morley, a widow of Lewes.

One of the principal points of her will ordered that the prior of the Cluniac order in Southover – the original site of the school – should be responsible for the nomination of 'a schoolmaster and usher to teach grammar therein for ever'.

For ever is a long time, but it is just feasible that, over the years, one of the nominees took this instruction absolutely literally.

Reading a poem in the latest edition of the school magazine, the idea struck me that the answer to the identity of the elusive visitor might lie among past pupils rather than staff. The poem was written by a VIth form pupil who was about to leave after 14 years – no less! – in the establishment. The last four lines are:

*It's very hard to leave you all
And better words I cannot find
Except to say, it's not these walls
But part of me I leave behind.*

Well, why not? It's as likely as any other theory!

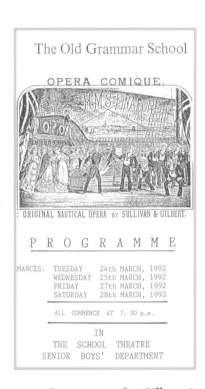

Above: Roy Mead with the Fifth Form, 1981–1982.

Below: Eileen Buckeridge with the third year girls, 1983.

Programme for Gilbert & Sullivan's 'HMS Pinafore', 1992.

Roy Mead with Sports Day winners in 1991

A MATTER OF TRUST

In 1989 Roy Mead took a bold decision designed to save LOGS from the sorry fate of many another private school at the time.

'People were asking what was going to happen in the future,' he explained. 'So many schools in the area were being sold off for building and development – Seaford had once had seven of them along the road to Eastbourne, and now there was only one left.

'I decided that I wasn't going to be the last headmaster of the school, so I set up a board of trustees and sold it to them.'

This wasn't retirement, since Mead was not quite sixty and fully intended to go on until he was sixty-five. It certainly wasn't a money-making wheeze either, for he had the buildings valued and sold them to the trustees for just 70 per cent of the market rate.

'I went along to the NatWest and said that I wanted to borrow £371,000 for the trustees so that they could pay me. The bank immediately said "fine", and for a very good reason – I'd paid back every penny I ever borrowed, and never defaulted once in more than thirty years.'

The four initial trustees, for the record, were Martin Costin of the solicitors Wynne Baxter; Jim Sweeney of the Uckfield accountants Swindales & Gentry; Julian Senior, a member of staff; and Ron Farley, one of the parents.

Mead now became their employee, and would remain so until his retirement in 1995, by which time the roll had risen from that modest 35 at his first assembly to a remarkable 420 – 250 in the senior school, 130 juniors and 40 sixth formers.

He would himself become a trustee in 1996, but performed one further act of generosity while he was still headmaster. In 1994 Tyne House at no. 140 came on the market, and he lent the trustees the deposit so that they could buy it. The sixth form moved there from the rooms above the Nationwide Building Society, and LOGS now occupied three houses in the row.

Tyne House is a Grade II* listed building, the earliest parts dating from around 1600. It was once owned by the Duke of Newcastle, who apparently used it to house one of his mistresses.

2000

Opening in London of the Tate Modern gallery, the Millennium Dome and the Millennium Bridge; Lewes suffers severe flooding as the River Ouse breaks its banks

2001

'Nine-eleven' terrorist attack on the Twin Towers, New York, and other targets; foot-and-mouth disease affects agriculture and tourism throughout Britain

2002

Death of the Queen Mother aged 101; Queen's golden jubilee

Right: The school anthem written by Roy Mead

NEW MEN AT THE TOP

The seventeen years from his retirement until the quincentenary were still very much part of the Mead era, as the previous owner continued to exert a strong influence on all aspects of life at LOGS, but three headmasters would lead the school towards that impressive anniversary.

The first was Dr Adrian Hodd, who in 1995 arrived from Charters Ancaster in Bexhill, where he had been deputy head. Just as Roy Mead had felt the need for change after the lengthy Cecil Lewis incumbency, so Dr Hodd applied himself to modernisation following the thirty-year Mead reign.

'It was a challenging time,' he recalled in his retirement. 'Not only was Roy Mead a hard act to follow, but money was very

SCHOOL ANTHEM

Chorus	'Floreat Lewys' be the call, The call be made with pride, The pride to carry with us all, Throughout the world so wide.
Verse 1	How beautiful, how wonderful! The sense of friendship feels. The power, the food, the very spur That turns life's varied wheels.
Verse 2	We live to learn and learn to live A thirst for knowledge see; Though each possess within his soul A deep humility.
Verse 3	The stage of life is set for all And those who tread it round Accomplish at the final fall The sweetest pleasing sound.
Chorus	Floreat Lewys be the call, The call be made with pride, The pride to carry with us all, Without thy walls so wide, Those many virtues which inspire . . . All men in God abide.

tight. After paying interest on our loans there was only a small profit each year, and that was ploughed back into the buildings, which were cramped and run-down. We developed the old squash court behind St Clair House into a DT room, and we also created a new library and an IT suite.

'There was fierce competition from other schools in the area, and we had to market ourselves like mad. We positioned LOGS as an academically sound day school at a modest price, and we set up scholarships, inviting bright pupils to apply.

'Becoming a member of the Independent Schools Association was an important step. To qualify we had to monitor the work of the staff to assess how good a job they were doing. Of course we had a pretty good idea already, but this was a formal process, and it was exhausting and time-consuming.'

When Dr Hodd stepped down in 2000, pupil numbers were little changed at about 400, but that competition was about to bite. During the two-year reign of his successor, David Cook, the roll fell to under 300 and the school found itself on a financial knife-edge. No fewer than twelve members of staff lost their jobs because of the urgent need to cut costs.

Above: David Cook.

Below: Dr Adrian Hodd (centre front, dark suit) with the sixth form 1998–1999. Several of his teachers were still at the school during the quincentenary year.

LOGS THROUGH AND THROUGH

Tim Laker first came to the school as a 7-year-old, later taught here and is today a trustee with special responsibility for overseeing the development of its buildings.

" It was April 1973 that I first entered the portals of 141 High Street. Little did I know then that the decision by my parents to send me to LOGS would be the start of a very enjoyable journey through the next forty years of the school's history.

I started in the junior school, in form C. I was very happy there, and made many friends, but I admit to having viewed the inevitable move to the senior school at 137 High Street with more than a little trepidation.

Roy Mead ruled the place with a rod of iron, although that didn't preclude us from what I can safely say was 'playing the game'. We studied hard, but also had great fun at the same time – often at the expense of others. There are many hilarious stories one could tell.

And then, out of the blue, I became a teacher. When I reached the sixth form, the technical drawing master left and wasn't immediately replaced. I was studying this subject, and I ended up not only teaching myself, but helping Mr Mead instruct the 'O' level groups in years 4 and 5. That year we had a 100 per cent pass rate!

I left in 1984 and went to study building construction at Brighton Polytechnic. A year later, Mr Mead asked if I was able to help teach the A-level pupils design on a part-time basis, and for two years I did that on two afternoons a week. It gave me the inspiration to think how I might develop my career and lecture at university at some time in the future.

I went on to train as a quantity surveyor. In 1992 I lost my job, and I was in Lewes, depositing my redundancy cheque at Lloyds Bank, when I bumped into Roy Mead. He invited me into the school and we chatted about old times. Asked if I was on holiday, I explained the situation I was in. After about two hours he said that he would like to offer me a job assisting Julian Senior, who was then the bursar, and teaching some geography and design. Little did I realise it at the time, but I had just gone through a very difficult interview!

I jumped at the chance and started at the beginning of the following academic year. I went on to take an MA in education at Sussex University, and rose to the dizzy heights of head of the boys' school and, eventually, director of studies.

In 2001 I decided to leave and return to quantity surveying. A mistake? At the start I suspected that it was, but three years later I was invited to become a trustee and to take on the responsibility of assisting with the building works planned for the coming years. When in 2010 I was made redundant again, the trustees asked me to take on the role of consultant and become operations manager for the school.

That decision for me has almost closed the loop, as one day I'm sure that I would like to return to the classroom. For the last few years I have been involved with 'master planning' the school, and in particular the senior department – although we also have in prospect a foundation unit for the juniors at Morley House.

As the quincentenary approached we were completing a new development at Mead House – building a new physics laboratory and geography room on the second floor, as well as providing new dining facilities and commercial kitchens. At the same time we were upgrading the facilities at Tyne House and St Clair House.

Working with English Heritage to get planning permission hasn't been an easy task. There was a period in our history during which several historical features were covered up, and our brief has been to reveal these architectural details and return the buildings to their appearance at the turn of the 1800s.

Mead House itself was designed as a school, but Tyne House and St Clair House were originally private residences. For me this is a magical moment: it's exhilarating and gratifying to restore buildings which have so much history.

I feel very privileged not only to have been part of the school's modern flowering as a pupil and teacher, but – in the role of trustee and custodian – to have been able to devote my energies to help reinforce the very foundations of this great institution as it marks its 500th year. "

Original drawing by Liam Russell Architects of the Mead House extension which opened in 2012.

2003

Americans and their allies, including the UK, invade Iraq, leading to the fall and capture of Saddam Hussein

2004

Devastating tsunami kills some 200,000 people following earthquake in south-east Asia

2005

Terrorist attacks on London tube trains and a bus, killing 52 people and injuring 700; Hurricane Katrina devastates US Gulf Coast

2008

Banking crisis leads to nationalisation of Northern Rock in the UK and large government stake in Royal Bank of Scotland

2009

Swine flu pandemic

2010

European sovereign debt crisis

2011

Arab Spring begins with fall of Tunisian government; massive earthquake in the east of Japan damages nuclear plants; wedding of Prince William and Catherine Middleton; Occupy movement spreads to more than 80 countries

BLEWITT BLOWS IN

The modern era at LOGS begins with the arrival of Robert Blewitt as headmaster in April 2003. He had been deputy head of an independent boys' boarding school in a leafy area of Surrey popular with professional footballers and their trophy wives, and at Lewes he found a different environment altogether.

'It was a bizarre interview,' he recalls now of his first visit to the school. 'It took place in Kit Wood's room. There were plants all over it, and books everywhere. They gave me a frail chair to sit on. I don't know whether that was deliberate policy, but it was almost collapsing when I sat on it and I did wonder whether it would survive intact until we'd finished.

'One question put to me, as a kind of test, was what I would do if the parents of a pupil who'd been declined entry for academic reasons offered to buy new facilities for the school in order to secure him a place.

'The right answer, which I eventually gave, was that it was vital to keep one's integrity rather than bow to financial pressure – but looking at the state of the buildings, it was easy to appreciate the temptation to take the money!

'The fabric was in a very poor state of disrepair, unbelievable. It seemed to me that people must have closed their eyes to it over a long period of time so that they simply couldn't see how bad it was.'

After the financial difficulties of the previous few years, and the letting-go of so many teachers, it wasn't suprising that morale was low, too. So what attracted him to the school?

'I've always said this,' he replies instantly. 'What I sensed immediately was its warmth, its soul. The staff and the trustees had a real love for the place and a caring attitude towards the pupils. It seemed to me, and I hope this doesn't have the ring of arrogance about it, that people were just waiting for a rallying round, for some leadership.'

Blewitt's first task was to stabilise student numbers, and that meant pinpointing what had been going wrong.

'Of course the general shabbiness must have put many prospective parents off,' he says, 'but buildings don't make schools. I felt the greatest failing was the lack of clarity in the promotional material the school was sending out. What exactly were we offering? The pupils were much more important than the fabric, and parents needed to know what would happen to their most treasured possessions if they entrusted them to our care.'

Many of the teachers were retained, with around 30 per cent still on the staff in 2012, but a new impetus was given to the arts and languages to match the existing excellence in maths and the sciences.

And the buildings? At that time the school was a company separate from the board of trustees (the two were incorporated in 2006), and it was vital to persuade the school's guardians to invest for the future.

Robert Blewitt at his desk.

'Rather like Stalin,' he smiles, 'I drew up a five-year plan, and I was grateful that the trustees accepted it. My hope was that within seven years – that is, by 2010 – LOGS would be what I regarded as the finished article. We haven't quite managed that, because my vision is probably still a couple of years away from being realised, but we have taken great strides.'

Those developments have included a new library, the teaching block at the back of St Clair House, a handsome sixth form centre, a new floor at Mead House and the refurbishment of the junior school at Morley House.

'What I'd still like to see,' the headmaster adds, 'is a proper performing area for drama and music, and – the crowning glory – the whole school being on one site. That's something we're working towards. Ideally we'll have more building at the back, overlooking the Paddock.

*The sixth form centre,
completed in 2010.*

'Lewes is a special place, and I hope to see us build new partnerships with other institutions in the town.'

As for student numbers, their early stabilisation soon gave way to a steady increase, until the trustees ruled that the impressive total of 500 reached in 2011–2012 must be regarded as the maximum – not principally because of the crush, but from a desire to retain the special intimacy of a small school.

'That's one of our attractions,' Blewitt says. 'Independent schools need to fill a niche. Some take in boarders, and some cater for boys or girls only. We've positioned ourselves as a relatively small co-educational day school with a challenging curriculum and a nurturing environment.'

A history of five hundred years survived through thick and thin is a great achievement. How does Robert Blewitt feel taking LOGS past that milestone?

'It's both a humbling experience and a proud one,' he says. 'You expect to take quite a few knocks in the academic world, and this is a rare moment to savour.'

Bibliography

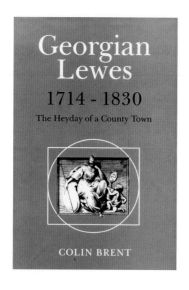

Brent, Colin *Pre-Georgian Lewes c890–1714* Colin Brent Books
Brent, Colin *Georgian Lewes 1714–1830,* Colin Brent Books
Caffyn, John *Sussex Schools in the 18th Century,* Sussex Record
    Society 81
Chapman, Brigid *The Schools of Lewes C13 to C21,* CGB Books
Crook, Diana (*ed.*) *A Lewes Diary 1916–1944,* Dale House Press
Dunvan, Paul *History of Lewes and Brighthelmston*
Ellman, Rev E. Boys *Recollections of a Sussex Parson*
Horsfield, T.W. *The History and Antiquities of Lewes*
Horsfield, T.W. *The History and Antiquities of Sussex*
Jewell, Helen M. *Education in Early Modern England,* Macmillan
Leach, A.F. *The Schools of Medieval England,* Methuen
Lower, Mark Antony *A Hand-book for Lewes;* various editions
Page, William (*ed.*) *Victoria County History,* vol 2
Poole, Helen *Lewes Past,* Phillimore
Salzman, L.F. (*ed.*) *Victoria County History,* vol 7

LOGS HEADMASTERS

(*from the move to St Anne's*)

1706–1725 Rev Thomas Peirce	1883–1893 Thomas Reader White
1725–1745 Rev Josiah Welby	1893–1895 Rev Henry Cruikshank
1745–1748 Rev John Bristed	1896–1904 Rev Dr Edward Hodgson
1748–1775 Rev Robert Austen	1905–1913 Charles Shepherd Smith
1775–1778 Rev James Castley	1916–1917 Rev H. Raymond Wansey
1778–1807 Rev William Gwynne	1917–1932 Rev Canon Evan Griffiths
1807–1821 Rev Edwin Merriman	1932–1933 David Vaughan
1821–1829 Rev Dr George Proctor	1933–1965 Rev Cecil Lewis
1829–1839 Rev Charles Williams	1965–1995 Roy Mead
1840–1848 Rev Dr James Cary	1995–2000 Dr Adrian Hodd
1848–1859 Rev Charles Green	2000–2003 David Cook
1859–1877 Rev Frederic Woolley	2003–present Robert Blewitt
1877–1881 Rev Charles Badgley	

Index

Part Two

THE QUINCENTENARY YEAR

The celebrations begin. On the evening of Sunday January 8, 2012 a dazzling fireworks display in the sky above Lewes heralded the LOGS 500th anniversary year. The fireworks were launched from the Paddock by Carnival Pyrotechnics of East Hoathly, and invited guests later attended a reception at the castle.

Pictured right are teacher Kit Wood flanked by Stephanie Gould and her son Russell, who left the sixth form in 2012, having been a pupil from reception.

LOGS Who's Who

Roy Mead

SENIOR SCHOOL
Headmaster: Robert Blewitt

Teaching staff:
Amoret Abis BA (Hons) PGCE: Art, Music
Brigid Argyle: BA (Hons) PGCE: PE
Nigel Ashford BA (Hons), PGCE: Practical Arts
Ivana Baric BSc (Hons) MSc: Chemistry
Robert Blewitt BA: Economics
Sally Blewitt: Library
Anna Brown BA Hons, PCGE: French, Spanish
Gillian Brown Cert.Ed. (Dist.): Mathematics
Mick Burgan Cert. Ed. MA Ed.: PE, Games
Magali Catucheau BA (Hons) PGCE: Spanish, French
Lucy Clougherty BA PGCE: English, Drama
Jane Dinmore BA (Hons), PGCE: Art, Graphic Design
Lynda Drunis Bsc (Hons), Cert.Ed MA Ed (Man.): Biology
Jenny Edwards BSc Econ (Hons), PGCE: Mathematics
William Ellis BA Geog (Hons), PGCE: Head of Year 8, Geography
Joanna Filmer BA (Hons), PGCE: Religious Studies
Tony Firmin BEd: Mathematics
Vivienne Frost BSc (Hons), PGCE: Physics
Derek Goss BEd (Hons) Cert.Ed: English
Shelley Griffiths BSc., PGCE: Mathematics, ICT
Liam Grove: Peripatetic music
Laura Hadfield BA (Hons), PGCE: History
Murray Heywood BA (Hons) PGCE: PE
Simon Heath B.Ed.(Hons), MA (LAE): Drama
Jessica Lloyd: Peripatetic dance
Christine Lowden BSc (Hons), MSc PGCE: Head of Science
Caroline Luker BSc (Hons), PGCE: Biology
Lynn Manning: Peripatetic Spanish

Robert Blewitt

Nigel Ashford

Derek Goss

Anne Pearce

Katy Pyper

Valerie Rosin

Kit Wood

Jose Matinez Pardo (BSc Hons): Science technician
Louise McCarron BA (Hons, joint) PGCE: English
Phillip McIver BSc (Hons): Head of Year 10, Biology
Astrid Masson Erste und Zweite Staatsprüfung: German, French
Lesley May Cert Ed: Home Economics
Rachel Munro BA (Hons): Singing
Mark Orchin Dip Mus (Open): Music
Anne Pearce BSc (Hons), PGCE: Head of Mathematics
Karen Peart BA (Hons), MA (CA), MA (IM): ICT
Genevieve Powney BA (Hons): English, Drama
Susana Prada Garcia BA, MA, PGCE: Head of Modern Foreign Languages
Ann Prior BSc (Hons), PGCE: Mathematics
Katy Pyper BSc, PGCE: Mathematics
Jonathan Rattenbury: Peripatetic music
Gemma Rham: English
Sam Rham: PE
Lucy Roberts BSc (Hons), PGCE: Head of Year 7, Physics
Valerie Rosin DEUG (French degree): Head of Year 12, French, German
Zoe Rye BA (Hons), PGCE: English, SENCO
Anna Scott B.Sc (Hons), MSc, D.Phil. PGCE: Chemistry, Biology, Physics
Lindy Smart Cert. Higher Ed.: Library and Information Science, Librarian
Henrieta Stefankova: Laboratory technician
Malcolm Strong: Laboratory technician
Louise Taylor BSc (Hons), PGCE: Chemistry
Melissa Thompson BA (Hons), MA: Head of English
Hannah Thorpe B.Sc. PGCE: PE, Dance
Debbie Ticehurst BEd. (Hons): Head of Year 9, PE, Psychology, Games, HE
Rebecca Townend BSc (Hons), PGCE: Geography
Peter Twilley BSc, PGCE: PE, Games
Richard Wakefield BSc (Hons), PGCE: Network manager, ICT
Paul Walton BA (Hons), PGCE: Head of Year 13, History
Louise Webster BA (Hons): PE, Dance
Gerwyn Williams MA (Hons) PGCE: Politics, RS, History
Natasha Witham MA (Hons): French, German, Spanish
Kit Wood MA (Oxon), PGCE: DT, History, Politics

ADMINSTRATION
Lynne Adsett-Knutsen, Finance manager
Nicki Prior, Finance assistant
Harpel Berry-Hill, Finance assistant
Kathryn Lake, Administration manager, PA to the head
Stephanie Gould, Business development manager
Tim Laker, Operations manager
Melissa Bibby, Transport, Administration
Gemma Scott, PA to the head, Morley House

JUNIOR SCHOOL
Head teacher: Guy Crossland

Teaching staff:
Victoria Bradford: Teaching assistant
Danielle Chapman BA (Hons) PGCE, Year 2 teacher
Mandy Duke BA (Hons): Reception class teacher
Gillian Dumbrell BEd (Hons): Deputy head, Year 3 teacher
Jessica Fracassini: Teaching assistant
Sue Giles NNEB: Foundation Stage co-ordinator, Nursery manager
Kathryn Gilderdale BTEC Nat. Dip./Early Years: Deputy Nursery manager
Elizabeth Glassey BTEC: Early Years practitioner, Reception class
David Gordon Cert.Ed.: Year 5 teacher
Louise Jackson BA(Hons): Year 5 teacher
Sarah Jago BEd (Hons): Year 6 teacher
Paulette Kemsley: Classroom assistant
Janice McKee BEd (Hons): Year 4 teacher
Christine Mitchell: SENCO assistant and dyslexia specialist
Gillian Noakes: Teaching assistant
Gemma Rham BA (Hons): PE
Sarah Richards BA (Hons), QTS: Year 1 teacher
Zoe Rye BA (Hons) PGCE: SENCO
Alice Shelbourn MA (Hons): Year 6 teacher
Angela Spinks Cert.Ed: Music co-ordinator
Julia Tucknott: Teaching assistant, Reception class
Carrie Whyte BA (Hons), PGCE: Year 4 teacher

SUPPORT STAFF
Sally Barnes (Kitchen)
Lisa Bertorelli (Kitchen)
Caroline Decaix (Kitchen)
Polly Fracassini (Catering manager)
Sarah-Jayne Hargreaves (Kitchen)
Greg Mitchell (Maintenance)
Sam Rham (Maintenance)
Debbie Russell (TA/Kitchen)
Amanda Taylor (Kitchen)
Kevin Thorpe (Driver)

Guy Crossland

David Gordon

Alice Shelbourn

Carrie Whyte

PUPILS 2011–2012

Edward Agnew, Nursery 1
Gracie Agnew, Year 1
Jawad Ahmed, Year 10
Tahmid Ahmed, Year 11
Florence Aldridge, Year 9
Ned Aldridge, Year 7
Joel Allaby, Year 9
Grace Allen, Year 8
Jess Allen, Year 10
Paige Allen, Year 10
Thomas Allen, Year 12
Tobias Allen, Year 10
Maximilian Andrew-Beale, Year 10
Moss Andrew-Beale, Year 8
May Andrews, Year 1
Skye Andrews, Year 3
Johnnie Arnold, Year 13
Jack Arscott, Year 13
Isaac Ayers, Nursery 2
Lauren Ayling, Year 8
Will Bacic, Year 7
Kirsty Bacon, Year 12
Alexander Baker, Nursery 1
Euan Baker, Year 9
Melissa Baker, Year 12
Alexander Baldy, Year 9
Matthew Ball, Year 11
Megan Ball, Year 12
Tristan Ball, Year 13
Joe Barber, Year 8
Miro Bardega, Year 7
Humphrey Barker, Year 10
Jack Barker-Gunn, Year 9
Somer Barlow, Year 9
Alice Barr, Year 12
Ellen Bartley, Year 11
Kathryn Bates, Year 10
Benjamin Battle, Year 5
Mia Battle, Year 1
Jacob Beauchamp, Year 9
Eliza Bell, Nursery 2
Mahira Bennetts, Year 12
Najoud Bennetts, Year 10
Zakaria Bennetts, Year 9
Eleanor Berryman, Year 10
Piers Berryman, Year 8
Caitlyn Biglands, Year 5
Reilly Biglands, Year 1

Charles Bird, Year 11
George Blackburn, Year 7
Christopher Bland, Year 11
Rebecca Bland, Year 13
Daisy Blewitt, Year 6
Jemima Blewitt, Year 3
Samantha Bolwell, Year 14
Alexander Bond, Year 9
Aran Borkum, Year 11
Kahina Bouhassane, Year 9
Kai Bowker, Year 10
Clara Boyland, Year 12
Emelia Boyland, Year 10
Alexander Boyne, Year 12
Richard Boyne, Year 10
Niav Bradford, Year 1
Kai Britt-Willows, Nursery 2
Leah Brooks, Year 8
Ben Brown, Year 4
Ella Brown, Year 7
Polly Brown, Year 4
Toby Brown, Year 2
Lucie Buchanan, Year 6
Matthew Buck, Year 10
Alexander Budnik-Grantham, Year 7
Alex Burdass, Nursery 1
Jack Cadogan-Rawlinson, Year 7
Daisy Canning, Year 11
Oliver Canning, Year 11
Ian Cardillo-Zallo, Year 9
Philip Carpinteiro-Olofsson, Year 6
Maya Carroll, Year 10
Sol Carroll, Year 8
Oliver Carter, Year 10
Nathan Casey, Year 8
Felicity Chadwick, Year 5
Olivia Chadwick, Year 8
David Charnock, Year 11
Belle Chippington, Year 11
Nick Chippington, Year 8
Jasmine Chitty, Year 8
Joe Chitty, Year 5
Alexander Chown, Year 7
Honor Clark, Year 8
Charlie Clarke, Year 11
Frederick Clarke, Year 6
Henry Clarke, Year 8
Polly Clarke, Year 6
Christopher Clay, Year 1
Zinnia Coates, Year 7
Millie-May Collins-Smith, Reception
Alfie Collison, Year 8

Bertie Collison, Year 3
George Collison, Year 12
James Cooke, Year 7
Henry Coomber, Year 10
Thomas Coomber, Year 7
India Cross, Year 7
William Cross, Year 9
Constance Crossland, Year 6
Nancy Crossland, Year 3
Phoebe Crossland, Year 9
Adam Crouch, Year 11
Bethany Crouch, Year 7
Daniel Crouch, Year 7
Ben Curran, Year 5
Niamh Curran, Year 9
Katia Damborsky, Year 11
Aria Darbahani, Year 7
Christopher Darbahani, Year 9
Alicia Davidson, Year 4
Jonny Davidson, Year 9
Tilly Davidson, Year 9
Jacob Davies, Year 11
Molly Davies, Year 7
William Davies, Year 9
Hebe Davies-Ratcliff, Nursery 2
Jemima Davies-Ratcliff, Year 5
Alexandra Davis, Year 10
Richard Davis, Year 7
Scarlett Dawes, Year 9
Jack Dean, Year 5
Ysobella Dean, Year 9
Alice Denning, Year 10
William Denning, Year 13
Clarissa Derrick, Year 2
Olivia Derrick, Year 5
Rebecca Derrick, Year 7
Harry Devonport, Year 8
James Dixon, Year 11
Lucinda Dixon, Year 13
Gabriel Dowsing, Year 9
Conor Doyle, Year 6
Rohan Doyle, Year 3
Guy Driver, Year 6
Alice Dryden, Nursery 1
Katherine Duffy, Year 10
Patrick Duffy, Year 7
Alexander Eastman, Year 8
India Edmonds, Year 9
Angus Elkins, Year 9
Eva Ellis, Nursery 1
Georgia Ellis, Year 5
Olivia Ellis, Year 1

Callum Elvidge, Year 8
William Elvidge, Year 11
Mark Evans, Year 10
Philippa Evans, Year 13
Maximilian Farkhad, Year 10
Alexander Boaler Farlie, Year 9
Benjamin Figg, Year 6
Rosanna Filmer, Year 10
Theodore Filsell-Bayes, Year 2
Amy Finnegan, Year 11
Alice Forsdick, Year 9
Olivia Foster, Year 9
Luka France, Year 11
Daisy Fretten, Year 6
Darcey Gallagher, Year 7
Gabriella Gallagher, Year 11
Maxim Gamble, Year 9
Freya Gandey, Year 11
Samuel Gandey, Year 13
Zoe Gandey, Year 10
Arman Gazeri, Year 9
Charlie Giles, Year 8
Harry Giles, Year 11
Inder Gill, Nursery 2
Jaskiran Gill, Year 2
Lawrence Gillians, Year 9
Lucy Gillman, Year 11
Jonathan Gilman, Year 13
Jennifer Goff, Year 10
Rebecca Goff, Year 11
Emily Goodman, Nursery 2
Jameela Gordon-King, Year 8
Oliver Gough, Year 1
Russell Gould, Year 13
Rory Graham, Year 10
Jack Grant, Year 11
Anna Green, Year 8
Ashli Green, Year 10
Edward Green, Year 5
Rachel Green, Year 5
Thomas Green, Year 9
Euan Gregg, Year 9
Glyn Griffiths, Year 3
Jazmine Griffiths, Year 2
Benjamin Griggs, Year 12
Maximilian Griggs, Year 9
Serena Guillemard, Year 7
Milly Hacker, Reception
Emily Hague, Year 8
Theo Haji-Michael, Year 5
Joseph Hajistylli-Bull, Year 11
Cameron Hardman, Year 7

Nicholas Harris, Year 12
Morgan Harrison-Holland, Year 10
Sophia Hart, Year 8
David Hartley, Year 10
Billie Harvey-Munro, Year 8
David Haw, Year 9
Emily Hawkins-Smith, Year 1
Holly Hawkins-Smith, Year 3
Oliver Hayden, Year 12
James Heaton, Year 10
Angus Heydon-Corrie, Year 8
Mirren Hicks, Nursery 1
Frederick Hoareau, Year 12
Daniel Holbrook, Year 7
Jonathan Holbrook, Year 5
Matthew Holbrook, Year 8
Lewis Hollebon, Year 8
William Holmstrom, Year 10
Hugo Hottinger, Year 9
Rory Hottinger, Year 11
Katy Hughes, Year 11
Lucy Hughes, Year 12
Pedrum Humphries, Year 8
Susanna Hunt, Year 7
Adam Hutchings, Year 10
Rhys Hutchings, Year 12
Jasmine Hyde, Year 4
Olivia Hyde, Year 7
Benjamin Ingham, Year 8
Oliver Ingham, Year 5

Ben Isaacs, Year 2
Elisabeth Jacobs, Year 10
Oliver Joergensen, Year 9
Philippa Joseph, Year 10
Riya Joshi, Year 9
Shamal Joshi, Year 11
Richard Kay, Year 10
Cerys Keating, Year 7
Khanasa Kiani, Year 11
Khayam Kiani, Year 12
Edmund Kirk, Year 8
Kars Koster, Year 5
Skip Koster, Year 1
Connor Lacey, Year 10
Finley Lacey, Year 8
Stan Lahood, Year 9
Jacob Lainchbury, Year 4
Anya Lawrence, Year 12
Kaira Lawrence, Year 9
Ben Ledingham, Year 7
Jack Ledingham, Year 9
Oscar Lees, Year 3
Summer Lees, Year 1
Gabriel Leggo, Year 6
Xavier Leggo, Year 2
William Lemonius, Year 10
Hannah Lewin, Year 8
Saskia Li, Year 10
Daniel Liddiard, Year 13
Joseph Light, Year 6

Warrior class: V. Campbell, the author of the novel Viking Gold, paid a visit to the school in January 2012.

Theodore Light, Year 2
Alexander Lindsay-Stewart, Year 11
Ella Lindsay-Stewart, Year 6
Christopher Linnell, Year 10
Robin Linnell, Year 7
David Livingston, Year 8
Salomon Livingston, Year 11
Celine Loh, Year 12
Nadine Loh, Year 11
Sophie Long, Year 10
Thomas Long, Year 10
Phoebe Longley, Year 11
Elspeth Lunt, Year 10
Iona Macdonald, Year 1
Toby Main, Year 10
Sophia Malik, Year 2

Yorke Manville, Year 11
Edward Marsh, Year 12
Madeleine Marsh, Year 7
Freya Maskell, Year 10
Willem Maskell, Year 12
Alexander Mason, Year 12
Emily Mason, Year 8
William Mawer, Year 10
Christopher Mayhew, Year 9
Peter Mayhew, Year 11
Tiarnan McCarthy, Year 11
Isaac McCloskey, Year 7
Elliot McGahan, Year 12
Joshua McGlone, Year 11
Laura McGuire, Year 8
Lawrence McKay, Year 13

Lucy Melville, Year 12
Benjamin Merritt, Year 12
Freya Merritt, Year 10
Kallan Millar, Year 9
Andrew Miller, Year 11
Joshua Miller, Year 6
Isabel Mills, Year 11
Katy Mills, Year 7
Liberty Mills, Year 10
Atticus Mohapi-Dobouny, Year 4
Alexander Morris, Year 11
Megan Morton, Year 10
Charles Moss, Year 11
Seyed Daniel Mousavi Zadeh, Year 13
Harrison Moy, Year 11
Esme Mukherjee, Year 7
Phoebe Mukherjee, Year 8
Matthew Mundroina, Year 12
Jamie Murray, Year 9
Maximillian Murray, Year 12
Samuel Murray, Year 12
Claudia Newton, Year 4
Jake Newton, Year 8
Joel Newton, Year 4
Natasha Newton, Year 6
Rowan Nichols, Year 7
Linus Nicholson, Year 11
Alexander Noakes, Year 5
Max Norville-Marwick, Year 11
Anna Nye, Year 6
Florence Oates, Year 11
Harry O'Brien, Year 8
Titus Ogilvie, Year 8
Riyadh Abu Omar, Year 5
Ella Orme, Year 7
Maia Orme, Year 11
Elka Overfield, Nursery 1
Nathan Packham, Year 8
Benjamin Page, Year 12
Rebecca Page, Year 8
Thomas Page, Year 7
Oni Palmer-Malthouse, Year 4
Stavros Paravas, Year 8
George Parnell, Year 12
Henry Parnell, Year 10
Ella Partington, Year 9
Avi Patel, Year 13
Dylan Patel, Year 6
Esha Patel, Year 5
Mya Patel, Nursery 2
Priyanka Patel, Year 10
Riti-Ekta Patel, Year 9

Love story: Dr Rosamund and Darren Clift, seen at the January reception which launched the anniversary year, met as students at LOGS. They became an item when sixth form students in 2003 (both were head prefects) and they married in 2011. Roz (née Partlett) qualified as a doctor in 2010, while Darren – a LOGS trustee – works for the local family business Tates.

Beri Pearce, Year 9
Elizabeth Pearce, Year 3
Fletcher Pearce, Year 12
Huxley Pearce, Year 4
Samuel Pearce, Year 8
William Pearce, Year 6
Luke Pelczarski, Year 8
Nicholas Perrin, Year 10
Lucy Petit, Year 3
James Pickford, Year 11
Katherine Pickford, Year 9
Amelie Pickup, Nursery 2
William Pile, Year 13
Arthur Plant, Year 10
Jonathan Platt, Year 10
James Pond, Year 13
Saphire Pond, Year 10
Andrew Porter, Year 8
Douglas Porter, Year 11
Hugh Porter, Year 5
Elizabeth Power, Year 12
Jake Power, Year 12
Ella-Louise Prior-McIntosh, Year 4
Elena Pryor, Nursery 2
Reece Pryor, Year 3
Phillippa Purnell, Year 1
Meeru Putland, Year 1
Daisy Quinn, Reception
Dirren Quinn, Year 3
Harry Rae Smith, Year 10
Charles Ramsay, Year 4
Emily Ramsay, Year 7
Louis Ramsey, Year 13
William Read, Year 7
Frederick Regan, Year 9
Felix Rentz, Year 4
Florence Rentz, Year 1
Alexander Restall, Year 10
Christopher Restall, Year 7
Finn Rham, Reception
Skylar Rham, Nursery
Maxwell Rhodes, Year 12
Bram Richards, Year 9
George Richenberg, Year 10
Theodore Richenberg, Year 8
Willow Rideout, Nursery 1
Phoebe Rivet, Year 10
Alexander Roberts, Year 2
Emily Roberts, Reception
Toby Robertshaw, Year 10
Carl Robinson, Year 13
Hannah Hunt, Year 9

Fenella Rowley, Nursery 2
James Rushton, Year 8
Farrall Ryder, Year 8
James Rye, Year 7
Dilhan Salgado D'Arcy, Year 10
Roshan Salgado D'Arcy, Year 12
Sara Salman, Year 7
Laura Salvage, Year 11
Samuel Sanders, Year 13
Amber Savage, Year 9
Alice Scott, Year 10
Beatrice Scott, Year 7
Christy Scott, Year 11
Jemima Scott, Year 10
Matthew Scott, Year 10
Kelson Sewell, Year 10
Rafik Shaheed, Year 13
Alexander Sharkey, Year 11
Hugo Sharkey, Year 9
George Shepherd, Year 11
Thomas Shepherd, Year 7
Archie Sherwood, Year 8
Matilda Sherwood, Year 13
Zachary Silver, Year 11
Jane Simmons, Year
Kitty Simmons, Year 7
Lily Simmons, Year 10
Robert Simmons, Reception
Sophia Simmons, Year 7
William Simmons, Year 9
Ezra Sinclair, Year 11
Philip Skeffington, Year 13
Guy Smart, Year 9
Madeleine Smith, Year 7
Natalie Smith, Year 11
Elliot Spencer, Year 6
Rosie Spencer, Year 8
Annabel Squire-Sanders, Year 9
Frederick Squire-Sanders, Year 7
Stephen Stanford, Nursery 1
Gemma Steer, Year 10
Paige Stein, Year 8
Tristan Stein, Year 9
David Stringer, Year 9
William Stringer, Year 8
Hector Summers, Year 2
Theo Summers, Reception
Dominic Swaine, Year 8
James Sweetman, Year 12
Isobelle Swinburn, Reception
Maxwell Swinburn, Year 3
Ella Swinney, Year 8

Jack Sywak, Year 9
George Taylor, Year 10
Benjamin Taylor Lovell, Year 10
Finley Taylor-Martin, Year 5
Lily Taylor-Martin, Year 2
Nicholas Telford, Year 10
Timothy Telford, Year 12
Arthur Thompson, Year 8
Tyra-Jayne Thompson, Year 13
Amelie Thorman, Year 2
Alexander Thornett, Year 5
Henry Thorns, Year 11
Millicent Thornton, Reception
William Thornton, Year 2
Kaan Thorpe, Year 10
Kaya Thorpe, Year 8
Oscar Thorpe, Year 8
Joshua Ticehurst, Year 11
Samuel Ticehurst, Year 8
Imogen Toomey, Year 13
Cengiz Topcuoglu, Year 5
Oliver Trimm, Year 13
Philip Tucknott, Year 11
John Tye, Year 9
Matthew Tye, Year 12
Nathan Umasankar, Year 7
Tamara Umasankar, Year 9
Thomas Van Howe, Year 5
Amelie Varennes-Cooke, Year 4
Madeleine Varennes-Cooke, Year 2
Callum Verity, Year 4
Toby Vernon, Year 9
Zoe Vernon, Year 11
Aaron Vincent, Year 9
Brooke Wain, Year 8
Harvey Waller, Year 11
Timon Walshe-Grey, Year 8
Toby Walshe-Grey, Reception
Willoughby Walshe-Grey, Year 4
Luka Watts, Year 10
Samuel Webb, Year 9
Beth Webster, Year 10
Finlay Webster, Year 2
Harvey Webster, Year 8
Ross Webster, Year 8
Amber Wells, Year 11
Emma West, Year 11
Myles West, Year 7
Catherine Westgate, Year 4
Harry Westgate, Year 2
Ruby Weston, Year 7
Robert Whippy, Year 13

Louis Whyte, Year 11
Theodore Whyte, Year 9
Jamie Wilkes, Year 13
Darcey Williams, Year 3
Dylan Williams, Year 5
George Williams, Year 9
Georgina Williams, Year 10
Hannah Williams, Year 5
Isabella Williams, Year 4
Oscar Williams, Year 9
Oscar Williams, Year 5
Thomas Williams, Year 12
Lucas Wilson, Year 11
Antonio Wingrove, Year 13
Freya Wish, Year 4
Scarlett Wish, Year 6
Thalia Witham, Nursery 2
Matthew Wood, Year 8
Michael Wood, Year 10
Lawrence Wright, Year 9
Oliver Wright, Year 11
Benedict Wye, Year 10
Samuel Wye, Year 7
Benjamin Young, Year 9
Jie Qiong Zang, Year 11
Cyrus Zargham, Nursery 2
Rafaella Zargham, Year 8

2012–2013 INTAKE

Michael Barker
Thomas Barry
Eden Bell
Rowan Bell
Thomas Bidwell
Luca Bish
Tarik Bouhassane
Emma Brooks
Alexa Chambers
Kiera Chambers
Vincent Clark
Jasper Conway
Jemima Cromby
Fyfe Davidson
Sophie Dawson
Billy Dean
Harvey Denness
Sophia Ferreira
Katy Finnegan
Alexander Fitzsimons
Eddie Flynn

Jonathan Gannaway
Harry Garoghan
Aryan Gazeri
Lydia Geary
Edwin Grove
Esme Higgs
Max Higgs
Ocar Hilton
Ben Isaacs
Maddy Issaacs
Tarr Jenkins
Yanbo Jin
Leon Keating
Sam Kimber
Georgina Lance
Paddy Leen
Howard Littlehales
Millie Long
Imogen Longley
Lewis Loudoun
Sarah Lunt
Henry Maurice
Oliver McDonald-Angear
Ross Merritt
Montgomerie Moorhouse

Joel Morris
Conor Morgan
Ella Ovenden
Louis Partington
Emily Pickford
Oliver Read
Tom Robinson
Bruce Rowley
Adrian Sahami
Samuel Sahami
Niloy Sil
Louis Soudain
Arun Spencer
Bonnie Steel
Ella Stevens
Fergus Tarr Jenkins
Ivy-Juliannia Terry
Layla-Beau Terry
Barry Thomas
Aaron Todd
Rebecca Todd
William Travers
Freddie Venturi
Drew Wain
Samuel White

A February highlight for the school was the visit of the author, actress and wildlife campaigner Virginia McKenna, seen here with Year 6.

Calendar of Events

IT BEGAN, FITTINGLY FOR LEWES, with a dazzling fireworks display, featured a showcase festival of visual and performing arts at Glyndebourne, a Founder's Day Parade through the town and a grand summer ball at Firle Place, and ended with a service of commemoration at St John sub Castro church. In between there were sports days, prize-givings, school visits and participation in the unrivalled Lewes bonfire celebrations.

The quincentenary year, in short, was a mixture of 'business as usual' and stand-out special events – and no one who played a part in the school's 2012 activities would ever forget it.

The Cliffe Drummers from Cliffe Bonfire Society making their vigorous contribution to the launch of the quincentenary year before the fireworks lit up the sky.

An inspector calls . . .

Early in the year the Independent Schools Inspectorate issued its report on LOGS following its visits during the previous November and December. Here are its findings in nutshell form:

• Pupils' learning and achievement is good throughout the school and is excellent in some areas of the senior school. These standards are fostered by a good curriculum which gives pupils significant experience in a wide range of subjcts.

* Pupils reach high standards and gain great enjoyment from a wide range of exta-curricular activities, including drama, music and many sports. Pupils benefit from good teaching from highly committed and knowledgeable teachers. Pupil-teacher relationships are excellent.

• The governance of the school is good, fulfilling all the legal requirements, supporting the steady improvement of standards and backing significant developments in the school as a whole.

• Parents of pupils of all ages are highly supportive of the school and its family atmosphere. Many commented that their children love going to school. Pupils particularly mentioned the way teachers care for them.

• Throughout the school pupils demonstrate excellent attitudes to learning: good behaviour, positive values, enthusiasm and excellent relationships, both with staff and between pupils.

• The junior school curriculum extends beyond the expectations of the national curriculum. Pupils greatly enjoy activities, including dance, netball, football and fitness clubs. Music is prominent, with a school choir, whole school productions and many pupils taking instrumental and singing lessons.

• The curriculum in the senior school has significant strengths, both in the range of subjects offered and in the way it is individualised to meet the needs of pupils.

• The quality of teaching is good throughout the school and enables pupils of all abilities to achieve a great deal.

• The personal development of pupils is excellent across the whole school, contributing much to the school's caring family atmosphere and reflecting the aims of the school.

• The trustees are very committed to the school, and a number have been parents, pupils or staff at the school.

• The quality of links with parents is excellent. The school has built on the good relationships noted at the time of the last inspection. One parent commented 'It is a privilege to be a member of the LOGS family.'

500 Festival

Lewes Old Grammar School
Celebrates 500 Years with our...

500 Festival

25th March 2012

GLYNDEBOURNE

Well over a thousand guests filled Glyndebourne opera house on Sunday March 25 for a song, dance and theatre extravaganza involving more than two hundred pupils. Visitors also enjoyed a display of the school's art and design & technology work.

The 19-act performance included pupils of all ages, and the talent on display included a juggler-cum-unicyclist, a folk ensemble and an all-male piece of physical theatre centred on Charlie Chaplin's bowler hat. In one charming performance, 'Dance When the Bell Goes', children from Morley House turned traditional playground games such as leapfrog and Granny's footsteps into a heart-warming dance routine.

Top: The performance of Adiemus by Karl Jenkins which opened the show was the first time that the LOGS Orchestra, the Vox Choir and Morley House pupils had performed together on a large-scale piece. The choir was conducted by Rachel Munro.

Left: In 'Sophie's Monologue', Sophie Long engaged in a bout of introspective soul-searching. This developed into whingeing self-pity, before being interrupted by . . .

Right: . . . the dancers of 'Oscillate Wildly' (Beatrice Scott, Molly Davies, Emily Ramsey and Madeleine Smith), who snapped her out of her navel-gazing with a bout of frenzied capering.

Above: 'Dance Charlie Chaplin', choreographed by Emma Larcombe and danced by senior boys.

Right: Getting ready to go onstage.

Below: 'Water is Wide'. Grace Allen sang the folk song, accompanied by senior school dancers and violinists Maxim Gamble and Ella Partington.

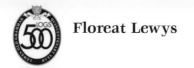

'Dance When the Bell Goes', choreographed by Jess Lloyd and performed by the Morley House dance club. Their playground games included (above) Granny's footsteps and (below) Ring-a-ring-a-roses.

Left: 'Drama Chairs', in which Year 8 girls engaged in an increasingly manic moving of chairs until, at last, they were satisfied with the arrangement and could leave the stage at ease with themselves.

Below: The LOGS Folk Ensemble. led by music teacher Mark Orchin. Left to right: Ella Partington, Maxim Gamble and Gemma Steer.

This way to the 500 Festival.

Below: In 'The Invisible Boy', devised and actedd by Freya Gandey and Matt Ball, a boy performs a series of show-off tricks without managing to attract the girl's attention – until he stumbles and she rushes to his rescue. Thumbs up at last!

'Dance Replica.' Part of a mixed bill with Replica Dance Company at Lewes Town Hall in 2011, this dance – choreographed by Hannily Bendell and Thomas Pickard – was reworked for twenty senior school dancers.

'Bugsy Malone.' LOGS senior school first performed this show at Pelham House, Lewes, in 2010. Casting it alone took six weeks – with lots of girls dressed up as male gangsters.

*Right: 'You Never Listen',
written by Simon Heath and
performed by Zoe Vernon and
Katia Damborksky, explored
the hopes and fears of two
girls about to leave school and
venture into the world beyond.*

*Below: A dramatic silhouette
from 'Bugsy Malone'.*

Above: 'Shakin' at the High School Hop.' More than fifty students (cast, band and backstage crew) were involved in the LOGS musical 'Grease'. For the 500 Festival the dancers enacted the high school prom.

Below: 'Dance After School'. Choreographed by Jess Lloyd and the senior school dancers, this piece explored the reasons students love and loathe school.

The Masque of the Red Death', a play by Alex Broun adapted from the Edgar Allen Poe tale, tells the story of Prince Prospero, who locks himself and a hundred friends in his castle to avoid a contagion known as the Red Death.

Year 10 GCSE drama boys performed the piece, which recreates Poe's terrifying tale through the use of multiple narrators, symbolic settings and physical theatre.

Left: 'Coffee and Cake' by Simon Heath, performed by Timothy Telford and Anya Lawrence, had the couple experimenting with changes to their over-the-top stage personas – before gratefully returning to the status quo.

Below: The LOGS senior school singers and dancers interpreted two pieces of music from the 'swing' era: 'Me and My Shadow' and 'Get Happy'.

The LOGS rock orchestra, comprising both students and staff, has become a major part of performing arts festivals and school concerts. At the 500 Festival they performed 'In the Midnight Hour' and 'We Are the Champions', with Alex Sharkey as the vocal soloist.

Above: 'Dance Perfect'. As part of their GCSE coursework, LOGS dancers chose 'Perfect' by Motionhouse as their project. For the Festival it was a combination of Year 10 work, supported by those who had performed it as an examination piece the previous year.

Below: 'That Capulet Girl.' Year 10 GCSE girls performed an imaginative play by Bruce Kane about love and men, as experienced by Shakespeare's heroines. That's Anne Boleyn's head on the table!

The grand finale, 'The Rhythm of Life' from the musical 'Sweet Charity, was performed by Senior Vox, Junior Vox, Morley House Choir, Staff Choir, LOGS Dancers and LOGS Orchestra.

More than a hundred students and staff took part in this final number – some singing, some dancing and some playing musical instruments.

LOGS artwork on display at Glyndebourne.

Ashton International College principal Joe Erasmus.

Out of Africa

Students and staff from Ashton International College in Ballito, near Durban, visited LOGS in April as part of a link forged between the two co-educational, independent schools the previous year, when a 46-strong Lewes party flew out to South Africa.

The idea is to exchange information about school life, local culture and heritage on a regular basis – and a treat for the visitors in the 500th anniversary year was a trip (below) to Brighton & Hove Albion's Amex stadium.

Headmaster Robert Blewitt explains how the South African connection came about:

'It took us a long time to find the right school in Africa with which to conduct a pupil exchange programme. Throughout 2009 several possibilities were contacted and rejected, until we eventually settled on Seaforth College in Ballito. It was broadly the same size as us, it was co-educational, it educated students from 3–18 and its ethos appeared similar to ours.

'The details were initially a little hazy, but the principle had been agreed: we would take a party of students to South Africa in February 2011, and then we would host a similar group as part of our 2012 celebrations. After the initial early flurry of emails had subsided, the link went progressively colder and we feared the worst – when we suddenly discovered that Seaforth College had been taken over by an organisation who were branching out from their home in Johannesburg into Durban.

'This led to my first contact with Joe Erasmus, the new principal of Ashton International College Ballito, and the plan started really taking shape. Ashton under Mr Erasmus was reborn, with an emphasis on four key attributes: it wanted its students to show Courage, Character, Spirit and Heart – qualities which we similarly hope *our* students develop.

'The link is strong and growing, and there is a real sense of camaraderie when our students mix. We are now planning our second visit in 2013, and all involved know that they are part of a special relationship which will lead to life experiences and rich memories that will stay with them for ever.'

Above: Elephant on LOGS safari in South Africa. [Photograph Will Pile]

Below: The main building of Ashton International College, Ballito.

The LOGS Coat of Arms

Local artist and former pupil Rupert Denyer was commissioned to create the school's first officially sanctioned coat of arms for the quincentary year. Rupert had had experience of working with the College of Arms before, creating the designs for a set of English stamps, so he was well aware that strict rules had to be followed:

Rupert Denyer self-portrait.

'I worked under the guidance of the Richmond Herald of Arms, Dr Clive Cheesman. The essential elements were the 'lion rampant' and the eight 'crosses crosslet', while the book was suggested as a symbol of scholarship.

'The first stage was to verify the school's history with the College of Arms, who don't take these things lightly, and then we discussed the unofficial shield we'd been using for many years. The crosslets represented Lewes Priory, and the overall design was similar to the arms of more than one great Sussex family, but a straight copy was out of the question – we were challenged to produce something unique that only LOGS could use.

'It was apparently thought that I would produce a white lion, but the herald was perfectly happy with the gold I chose. What he did insist on was that the beast's teeth, tongue and claws should be blue, as should the medieval book, which was to be quarter-bound with gold corners and metal clasps.

'That sounds pretty prescriptive, but I could otherwise create whatever kind of lion I wished. We decided that it should be "bas relief" in form, and then I just got on with it – and enjoyed myself immensely! This type of commission doesn't come along very often. It was wonderful to work on such prestigious and unusual project, and the fact that it was for my old school was an added bonus.

'I even created my own typeface for the motto underneath. The *Floreat Lewys* scrollwork isn't part of the official coat of arms, but of course the school will always use it in conjunction with the shield.'

The blazon of the Lewes Old Grammar School coat of arms is described as follows: 'Murrey within an Orle of eight Crosses crosslet Argent a Lion rampant Or holding in the forepaws a Book bound Azure edged garnished and the spine Or.'

'Murrey' is the heraldic name for mulberry coloured, or reddish purple. The other colours are silver (argent), gold (or) and blue (azure).

The shield echoes the device of the old borough of Lewes – said to combine the arms of the Fitzalan family (dukes of Norfolk) with crosses to represent Lewes Priory – but there are similarities, too, with the arms of the de Braose and De La Warr families.

The granting of the LOGS coat of arms was conveyed to the trustees by means of a large vellum document recording the school's history.

Founder's Day Parade

Lewes was taken back in time for the Founder's Day Parade through the town on Friday May 25, with Morley House pupils modelling the clothes children would have worn in 1512, 1612, 1712, 1812 and 1912, and others sporting costumes depicting famous people or events in the school's and the town's history.

The senior school carried banners demonstrating changes in education over the five centuries, some students bringing the pageant up to date by wearing 2012 sports strip and other gear.

After the parade – from the Paddock and back again, via the High Street – LOGS put on an afternoon of entertainment, having invited anyone involved with the school to join in the fun. The story of the day is told by English teacher Derek Goss.

"It was five hundred years ago that Agnes Morley endowed her school for the children of Lewes and five centuries later, on a sweltering May afternoon, the newest generation of that school, appropriately now over five hundred in number, processed through the streets of the town.

Had Agnes Morley been alive to take part in this procession there would have been much about the old town she might well have recognised, but quite what she would have made of the children who attend her school today would be a matter of speculation.

James Rushton and Kit Wood leading the tableaux with a banner of the LOGS 500 emblem.

What she would have seen was a school with a sense of community and a joyous attitude in their approach to their education – this procession reflected a school which pupils are not only happy to attend, but also one in which they are fully involved.

The procession was led by the town mayor followed by Henry VIII and his wife who bore a remarkable resemblance to the current head, Robert Blewitt and his wife – whether his wife was Anne Boleyn or one of the luckier survivors is a matter for conjecture, but being in Lewes one might assume Anne of Cleves.

Other notables in the procession included junior school teacher Sarah Jago dressed as Agnes Morley; King Charles (or was it Brian May of Queen?) cunningly disguising the features of Junior School Head, Guy Crosland; Kit Wood, one of the longest serving members of staff as an early twentieth century pupil, complete with 'topper'; and various current staff members adorned with gowns and mortar boards.

The town of Lewes was brought to a standstill, with roads shut to enable the parade to proceed on its journey and members of staff acting as road stewards to ensure public safety. This was all co-ordinated by Mr Wakefield, loaded down with so much technology that had he fallen over he would never have got up again; but nonetheless ensuring everything went without a hitch.

As the procession wound its way through the town, its presence was signalled from a distance by the sound of the brass Oompah Band, which included former head prefect, Sam Pearce. They were followed by students from the school representing the truly wide range of activities now offered to pupils at Lewes Old Grammar.

We had dance groups and cheerleaders, who certainly made Lewes aware of their presence through both costume and the volume of their chanting. Drama was represented by members of the casts of the two plays performed in this quincentenial year, 'Grease' and 'Daisy Pulls It Off'. Sports teams representing rugby, football, athletics and hockey looked smart in their various school kits. The success in the sports field by many of our students is a testament to what can be achieved by a relatively small school when the commitment is whole-hearted.

Top: Tim Laker keeping his head as Charles I.

Bottom: Science teacher, Phil McIver.

The Junior School provided one of the most colourful spectacles of the afternoon when the youngest children in the school, ranging from nursery to Year 6, paraded in children's costumes through the ages. Tudor children marched with their contemporaries from Georgian and Victorian generations and twentieth century pupils from the new Elizabethan Age. The costumes were vivid and colourful, highlighting the tremendous amount of work from Mrs Tucknott and her band of helpers.

One of the important aspects of life at Lewes Old Grammar is its association with life in the town itself. This was clearly illustrated by the spectacle of The Cliffe Drummers from Cliffe Bonfire Society marching in the parade with various members of the Williams family, all current pupils of the school. Again a sense of history was in evidence: Lewes' long tradition of bonfire celebrations dates back to events at the time of the Gunpowder Plot in 1605 and the burning of the Lewes Martyrs beginning in 1555, a mere thirty-seven years after the founding of the grammar school!

Right: Tableaux on the march, with the school beyond.

In case anyone was wondering whether any academic work now takes place at the school, a display of banners reflecting the various subject areas of the curriculum represented this aspect of LOGS life. The CDT department had created an ingenious presentation of such diverse subjects as a global view of the world in 1512 and 2012, a display of stringed instruments through the ages and a series of strange and weirdly shaped objects that only a mathematician could think up, and possibly understand.

Having made its way through the town, the parade reached the Paddock, where further activities and refreshments were laid on for pupils, parents and guests. Many former members of the school were present to swap memories and recall their time there. Music was provided by a number of the school musicians and bands, and the Paddock reverberated to their sound. Whether Agnes Morley would have turned in her grave or rock 'n' rolled with the best will never be known, but it would be nice to think the latter.

Above: A young GI represents the 20th century.

Below: The procession nears the Paddock.

In the spirit of returning to the past, a maypole was set up and many children were involved in a strange version of this ancient custom, which in its twenty-first century guise appeared to consist of wrapping Mrs Smart, the librarian, around her own kindly donated pole!

This was a memorable day in the history of the school which has celebrated many fine achievements during its long history, but perhaps the spirit of the occasion and of the school itself could best be summarised by a quotation on the 'English' academic banner from a famous old boy and diarist, John Evelyn: Friendship is the golden thread that ties the hearts of all the world. **"**

Above and right: Music and munch at the Founder's Day Paddock event.

Summer Ball

The summer ball at Firle Place in July was a black-tie event which brought together more than 300 current and past teachers and students. Afterwards there was a magnificent fireworks display in the grounds, followed by dancing first to the LOGS rock band and then to a local group, The Ice Cream Bikinis.

Left: the room ready for the guests, and the meal about to start.

Above, top: It rained heavily for much of the evening, but school secretary Kathryn Lake and her husband John came prepared. The rain cleared before the fireworks display.

Below: Best bib and tucker included a fine bowler hat worn by parent Joe Light.

Above: The snapper snapped.

Left and below: the magnificent firework display during a fortuitous pause in the heavy rain.

Swinging to the sounds of the Ice Cream Bikinis at Firle Place.

Junior Sports Day

Scenes from a fun-packed June afternoon at the Paddock

Senior Sports Day

Action and awards at the athletics track in July

Facing page, clockwise from top left: Freya Merritt in the Year 10 girls' long jump; Will Bacic winning the Year 8 boys' 100m; Year 10 girls' house relay; Riya Joshi gets the discus wrong; and Jamie Cooke holds his head in despair.

This page: England international 3000m steeplechaser Rob Mullett presents the prizes. Clockwise from top left: Hannah Rose and Will Davies receive the cup for the winning house, De Montfort; presentation to junior boys' Victor Ludorum winners, Kallan Miller and Ian Cardillo-Zallo; senior Victor Ludorum Jake Power; intermediate Victor Ludorum James Heaton; and intermediate Victrix Ludorum Emelia Boyland.

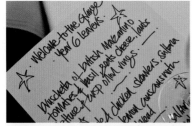

Year Six leavers

A celebration at the Grange

Sixth form ball

*A lively evening at the Grange
with food provided by Bill's of Lewes*

Junior Prizegiving

Awards ceremony at the town hall

Trophy winners, clockwise from right: Milli Thorman, Citizenship Cup; Eddie Green, Courtesy Cup; Dylan Patel, Progress Cup; Polly Clarke & Holly Hawkins-Smith, Dance Cup.

Clockwise from top left: Emily Roberts, Reception Creative Trophy; Huxley Pearce, Year 4 Creative Cup; Polly Brown, Year 4 Academic Trophy; Joseph Light & Daisy Fretton, Outstanding Achievement Cup.

Top to bottom: Head teacher Guy Crossland; Xavier Leggo, winner of the Year 2 Creative Cup; and Sports Girl of the Year Connie Crossland.

The 2011–12 prefects team, top to bottom: Head prefect Will Pile; head girl Tilly Sherwood; head boy Sam Gandey.

Russell Gould holding the Laker shield for design and Amy Finnegan with the Trier Cup for modern languages.

Prize-winners for Years 7–9.

Sporting achievements: Emelia Boyland, winner of the Victrix Ludorum cup and hockey player Harvey Waller with the Sportsman's Salver.

Senior Prizegiving

Awards ceremony at the town hall

Ben Griggs with Taffy's Spade for service to the community.

The Year 13 academic award was shared between Lawrence McKay (left) and Jack Arscott.

The new team: Head prefect for 2012–13 Lucy Melville and head boys George Parnell and Roshan Salgado D'Arcy.

The Whole School Walk

Every year the staff and students walk from the school to Stanmer and back – some in fancy dress – to raise money for charity.

The 2012 walk, in September, raised some £6,000 for Fish Aid (the Anthony Pilcher Bone Cancer Trust) and Amos Trust (Umthombo Street Children of Durban, South Africa)

Roy with his daughters and son-in-laws, Alison and Ray Davies (left) and Frances and Jake Keogh.

The school hall transformed for the evening.

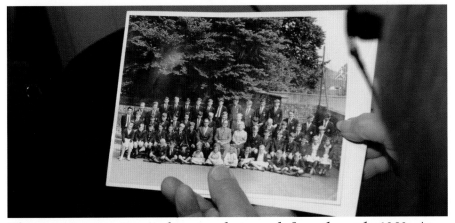

The way we were: Roy is shown a photograph from the early 1960s, in which he sits next to his predecessor as headmaster, Cecil Lewis.

Fifty years on

*A tribute evening was arranged in September 2012 to mark Roy Mead's 50 years as a teacher, head/proprietor and trustee.
The invited guests included many former pupils, teachers and trustees.*

Roy Mead presented the school with portraits of himself and his late wife Isabel, painted by local artist (and former pupil) Rupert Denyer.

His verdict: 'It was a wonderful evening – so much so that it was difficult to persuade people to leave!'

Morocco bound

October 2012 saw the school's 11th trip to Morocco. Now a regular event in the calendar, it was first inspired by the then head of geography, Liz Williams, back in 1990.

The 2012 expedition involved eleven Year 13 students. It was led by William Ellis, Kit Wood and Tim Laker, who here jointly recall the beginnings of the enterprise, report on the latest visit and reflect on its value to those lucky enough to experience it.

"In the early days the flight was from Heathrow via Casablanca to Marrakech. On that first trip a group of sixth formers spent three days studying land use, agriculture and the environmental impact of a migrating population. The second half of the week was spent in Imlil, a High Atlas village in the valley below Jebel Toubkal, which (at 4167m) is the highest peak in North Africa.

On a subsequent trip Liz Williams and Tim Laker discussed a possible link with a Moroccan school. Their trip leader from Discover Ltd made contact with a lycée in Tahananoute, a town in the foothills of the High Atlas. An official link was made between the two schools and the first trip was made by LOGS to the lycée in 1997. Together, students studied the geography of Imlil and the surrounding villages.

On their return, various fund-raising activities ensued, such as sponsored activities and a Morocco-themed evening. Despite visa problems, which for a time threatened to scupper their progress, students from Tahananoute visited Lewes in 1998 and 2001, hosted by both teachers and families. These involved local cultural and geographical visits, as well as excursions to London and Sussex University.

The 2012 group in the malodorous tanneries at Marrakech.

The 2012 expedition brought to over 150 the total number from LOGS who have visited this fascinating country. Needless to say, huge changes have been observed, as development has progressed. After a two-day stay in Marrakech, time was spent in Imlil, Ouarzazate and Zagora (fifty-two days by camel from Timbuktu). Highlights included sightseeing and bartering in Marrakech, culminating for the hardened few in sampling local delicacies such as sheep's head in the Jemaa el Fna on the last night.

Treks in the majestic Atlas Mountains were punctuated by the pre-Islamic 'sheep-man' festival (to mark Eid): in addition to heavy partying, this involved the donning of the fleece of a freshly-sacrificed ram by a village elder and the chasing of small children. The camel trek from Zagora irritated hitherto under-used muscles and proffered the now customary 'never again' response.

In one sense, the school's link with Morocco has been one-sided. It has been hard to raise the funds, find suitable times and battle the bureaucrats to bring our Moroccan friends and their students to Britain. This situation is not about to improve, as it is now necessary for every Moroccan citizen travelling abroad to visit Rabat in person and apply for a visa which will cost €300.

There is no doubt about the value of our students' visits to this fascinating kingdom. The picnics unloaded from mules and served under a sky of wheeling choughs in sight of snow-capped peaks; the palm groves and vegetable gardens in the Draa oasis under a cobalt sky; the campfire and haunting Berber music; the sensory and cultural kaleidoscope of Marrakech; the warmth of the people – these and many more riches are difficult to match in any other short visit.

We are, therefore, determined to forge ahead with the Morocco link. Currently under discussion, in addition to ongoing contact with our friends in Tahananoute, is the option of a new link with the Discover-based 'Education For All Morocco' charity (http://www.discover.ltd.uk/morocco/efam/). This will ensure that we give something back, in return for the generous, even sacrificial, hospitality so many of us have been privileged to enjoy.**"**

Liz Williams on one of the early trips.

The mosque of Koutoubia, Marrakech.

Out with a bang!

LOGS returned to its Southover roots on November 5th, taking part in the Southover Bonfire Society celebrations. LOGS banners depicted the geographical globes of 1512 and 2012 together with models of the original school and Mead House.

The first procession, to the war memorial at the top of School Hill, culminated in a short ceremony of remembrance, with wreaths laid on behalf of the school's alumni.

In the United Grand Procession the school marched behind the LOGS 500 banner in period costumes from 1512 to the present.